FOLK REVIVAL

The rediscovery of a national music

FOLK REVIVAL

The rediscovery of a national music

Fred Woods

BLANDFORD PRESS

POOLE   DORSET

First published 1979
© 1979 Blandford Press Ltd
Link House, West Street
Poole, Dorset, BH15 1LL

ISBN 0 7137 0970 7   (Hardback)
     0 7137 0993 6   (Paperback)

British Library Cataloguing in Publication Data
Woods, Fred
  Folk revival.
  1. Folk-music, British – History and criticism.
  I. Title
  781.7'41   ML3560

Printed in Great Britain by
Fletcher & Son Ltd, Norwich

Contents

For

my Father and Burdette

in gratitude

Introduction

It is, I must confess, with some trepidation that I offer these interrelated essays on that musical phenomenon known as the Folk Revival. This is a first book on the subject and, as such, it cannot be other than a preliminary study. To attempt a full-scale investigation of all the movement's ramifications would, in any case, have involved a book of uncommercial dimensions and cost.

These are, then, a series of explorations of various aspects of the Revival; not a formal history of the folk movement, nor an authoritarian statement of facts, but rather a collection of my own thoughts and feelings, developed from a wide experience inside the Revival as journalist, record producer, broadcaster and editor.

Knowing the folk world as I do, I can anticipate only too clearly some of the criticisms: I haven't mentioned So-and-so, surely Such-and-such is far more important than Thingummybob. And so on. Maybe such criticisms are right, but any attempt to mention *everybody* (even including old So-and-so, the old so-and-so) would have made the book look like a mere list of runners and starting prices; and relative importances are, in any case, always a largely subjective matter.

A small amount of repetition will be found between one or two chapters; *some* recapitulation has been necessary, and I hope you will bear with its occasional appearance. Also, some parts of this book have already appeared (though in different form) in the pages of that excellent magazine *Folk Review*, to whose Editor (myself) I offer my grateful thanks for his permission to reprint.

In due course, doubtless someone will write the definitive history of the Revival, but that cannot really take place until the Revival itself is dead – if die it must. In the meantime, I offer this introduction to the folk world as a small return for the countless hours of enjoyment it has already given me.

F.W., 1978

Acknowledgements

While no one else can be blamed except myself for any opinions expressed in this book, I would like to thank the following people for many stimulating and helpful discussions: Harvey Andrews, Alex Atterson, Peter Bellamy, Alex Campbell, Bob Copper, Graham Cooper, Tony Engle, Dick Gaughan, Guy Lambrechts, Bill and Helen Leader, Ewan MacColl and Peggy Seeger, Michael Grosvenor Myer, Peter Pilbeam, Barry Seddon, Cyril Tawney and Mike Yates. Many others, too numerous to mention individually, have also contributed to my thoughts and will, I hope, accept my general thanks.

Photographs are reproduced by kind permission of Brian Shuel, Lothar Schiffler, Janet Kerr, Jim Jackson, John Bryan, The Decca Record Company Ltd., Simon Nicol, Warner Bros., Logo Records and Tony Fisher. Extensive checks have so far failed to identify the photographer of Charlie Wills.

Part 1
The Tradition

Folk Studies Since the Death of Cecil Sharp

The end of the nineteenth century and the beginning of the twentieth saw an enormous amount of activity by folksong collectors such as Sabine Baring-Gould, John and Lucy Broadwood, Frank Kidson, Mrs Milligan Fox, Mrs Kennedy Fraser, Mary Neal and, above all, Cecil Sharp. A slightly younger group of collectors included the composers Ralph Vaughan Williams, Percy Grainger, George Butterworth, E. J. Moeran and Herbert Hughes.

For previous generations, the music of the working class had been shut off from their 'betters' by the strong class barriers. The squires, parsons and landowners generally were simply unaware of the wealth of song available to their workers, since there were few occasions when they could meet it. It took an unusually inquiring mind, such as Baring-Gould's, or pure accident, such as led to the meeting of Sharp and the gardener John England, for contact to be made. But once the seeds had been sown, the harvest was rich. Hundreds of songs were collected and printed, usually with piano accompaniments and frequently adapted away from the modes in which they were sung; to the Victorians the modes sounded wrong, and they found it hard to believe that untutored labourers would instinctively sing modally.

But, while an immense treasure was recorded for posterity, it is fair to say that much of the earlier work was done in a spirit of amateur dilettantism, and certainly with a wholly antiquarian outlook. In the shrinking rural culture with which they were faced, the collectors believed that they were saving the songs from an inevitable oblivion, and their work was therefore governed by an archaeological approach. As late as 1923, in his *Folk Songs of the Upper Thames*, Alfred Williams wrote: 'The songs themselves, as far as singing goes, are practically defunct. There is no need to revive them. To do so, in fact, would be impossible. It is also undesirable. We live in a new age, almost in a new world. Life has changed. There are other amusements. We move at a quicker pace . . . Let us, then, be content to say that folk-song is dead. But we want to preserve the words, not for their artistic or strictly literary value, but in order to have records of that which amused, cheered, consoled, and so profoundly affected the lives of the people of an age that has for ever passed away.'

Certainly the Industrial Revolution had done much to shatter rural life in a variety of ways, and old traditions were falling into disuse. That they were soon to be given an almost more serious blow in the shape of World War I was, of course, hidden to them; but they imagined that the old life had gone for ever. It is, perhaps, surprising that none of the collectors thought to inquire if the Revolution had created its own songs and traditions; but as the continuing creativity of the tradition was not understood there was presumably no incentive to look for new examples.

So the main emphasis of the research of this period was not so much on recording the traditional songs and dances *per se*, as saving them for the delectation of the upper and middle classes – inevitably so, since the working classes seemed to have jettisoned them, and it was up to their 'superiors' to appreciate their beauty. To this end, many of the songs were published in drawing-room arrangements, and the frank bawdry of folk-song was discreetly rewritten for delicate ears. Fortunately one or two collectors – Baring-Gould among them – kept the original words in their notebooks for future generations.

But, and possibly more serious than the bowdlerisation, the early collectors also imposed a middle-class (and antiquarian) view of what actually constituted folksong. Many songs in the singers' repertoires were ignored as not being 'traditional'; songs from the music hall and the popular songs of the day were simply not collected. The fact remains, though, that even if they were not 'traditional', they were sung by traditional singers, and their arbitrary exclusion has cast a distorted light on the picture which still lingers on today. Not only was the repertoire censored, but the whole function of the traditional singer was misunderstood and misinterpreted. To judge by the printed output of the time, the village singers offered a heady diet with a strong emphasis on the big ballads – a picture of altogether too arcadian perfection to be credible. A hard line was drawn between the traditional and the rest (which was, of course, at least *potentially* traditional), a hard line that was too often backed up by no more than sentiment and generalisation.

In *English Folk Song: Some Conclusions* (1907), Cecil Sharp wrote: 'The folk singers of today . . . are the last of a long line that stretches back into the mists of far-off days. Their children were the first of their race to reject the songs of their forefathers. Nowadays, the younger generations despise them, and, when they mention them, it is with a lofty and supercilious air and to pour ridicule upon them. The old singers, of course, hold the modern songs in like contempt, although they accept the changed conditions with a quiet dignity, which is not without its pathos. One old singer once said to me, "Our tunes be out o' vashion. They young volk come a-zingin' thicky comic songs, and I don't know they, and they won't hearken to my old-vashioned songs." '

Now I simply do not believe this. In the first place, it implies that folksong has always consisted of an unvariable, fixed repertoire, which has never been augmented or transmuted throughout its history. It also implies that folksong ossified at some unspecific point in its history – or, even more unbelievably, it ossified at an immaculate conception. Sharp's statement represents not only a gross misunderstanding of the development of folksong, but also a sentimental siding with the older generation. But the Napoleonic songs had come into being less than a hundred years before Sharp began collecting, and the industrial songs were still being written. So what's the definition of an 'old fashioned song'? Sharp wants us to believe that it's a traditional song but, even by his own tenets, recently written songs were being sung and handed down orally, the later murder broadside songs among them. And, by the same token, were instrumental accompaniments old-fashioned or new-fangled? There must have been a time when instruments were used for the first time ('I don't hold with thicky new-vangled viddles'), when fiddles and later melodeons and concertinas took over from pipe and tabor. Even traditional folksong has its developments. Slow, gentle and gradual they may have been, but developments there doubtless were, and have continued to be. The view of Sharp and his contemporaries that folksong was dead, and had died in just the generation when they started collecting, was implicitly self-destructive.

Vaughan Williams and, to a greater extent, Percy Grainger, were not so dogmatic. Grainger especially was keenly alive to the vitality of folksong, to the ever-changing detail and the shifts of personal contribution to old songs. Grainger alone among the collectors of his day saw that performance was a potent factor in the continuity of traditional music; he alone insisted on the importance of collecting not just the 'average' melody, but also the subtle variations put into a song by a skilled traditional singer. And, to intense opposition by the more conservative collectors, he advocated the use of recording equipment as the basic collecting tool, using pen and ink in a merely supporting role. He also struggled with – though never entirely conquered – the problem of creating an adapted notational system to cope with the embellishments and slides beyond the scope of the standard keyboard notation. In this respect, however, the recorder – however primitive – was clearly essential since, when slowed down, it could reproduce fast and complex decorations at a sufficiently slow speed to be deciphered.

But Grainger's was a voice crying in the wilderness, and he eventually departed the ranks of the collectors for other musical directions, leaving behind him some very ruffled feathers. As John Bird wrote in his biography of Grainger (1976), his approach 'threatened to expose the frequently hit-or-miss and sometimes dishonest techniques of other collectors. Grainger had little faith in the pencil-and-pad approximation of his contemporaries.'

It is a pity that a man of Grainger's brilliance should have moved on to other things (at the time of his death in 1961 he was involved in electronic compositions that pre-dated the Electric Light Orchestra and Rick Wakeman by more than ten years) for the face of collecting and folk studies might have been considerably different; there might, indeed, have been no need for a Revival.

Sharp died in 1924, and from then until the early 1950s little collecting work was done. One small event, however, had indicated that all was not yet lost: the discovery by E. J. Moeran, in 1921, of Harry Cox, an

East Anglian farmworker with a remarkable hoard of songs and a dry, understated style of singing. In the following year, some of his songs began to appear in the English Folk Dance and Song Society *Journal*, and ten years later the Society issued two of his songs on their first gramophone record.

In spite of the richness of this discovery, Cox was not visited again until after World War II. Conditions in the thirties were scarcely conducive to folksong collecting – there were other, more crucial, problems – and the first half of the forties also presented its own priorities. Folksong, as far as the general public was concerned, relapsed into a genteel drawing-room entertainment, and remained there until the Axis had been disposed of. But, as the presence of Harry Cox had hinted, the tradition was by no means dead. Quietly, self-effacingly, in villages and towns, farms and factories, the songs went on being sung.

In the early 1950s, the work of collecting began again with renewed vigour, and the first stage of the Folk Revival – but so far unrecognised as such – commenced. Without question, the credit for the initiative of this early work must go to the BBC, without whose vision and resources much might have been lost. As it was they caught the older traditional singers just in time: Harry Cox, George Maynard, Charlie Wills, Sam Larner and others were all around the seventy mark. But the effort of the BBC collectors and producers was herculean, and the fruits are still available and, in the case of the actual recordings, still appearing in LP or cassette form.

Country Magazine, for instance, played a traditional song in every programme, and Francis Collinson's *The Postman Brings Me Songs* presented material found as a result of people writing in to *Country Magazine*. And finally, *As I Roved Out* presented the findings of various collectors working all over the British Isles, though the bulk of the research was done by Peter Kennedy, Seamus Ennis and Bob Copper. This last programme emphatically proved the continuance of the English tradition, even if, at that stage, most of the singers discovered were undeniably elderly. (As to the Irish and Scottish traditions, they had never been lost, so the approach was not so much one of discovery and revival as of representation and reminder. The Celtic races, indeed, have always managed to retain their folk arts as a part of everyday life, and in the context of this book, the term 'Revival' should be regarded only as a convenient blanket term when applied to them.)

By this time, of course, the controversy about recording was long dead. Collectors all over the world, from Bartok down, had followed Grainger's lead and, in the context of *As I Roved Out*, recordings were essential anyway. Machines had much improved, though they were still heavy and cumbersome; the day of the handy and ubiquitous cassette was still far off. For the first time, then, recordings were acquired on a fairly massive scale. Bob Copper's excellent book *Songs and Southern Breezes* (Heinemann, 1973) describes his part in this operation with rich understanding; and Peter Kennedy's massive *Folk Songs of Britain and Ireland* (Cassell, 1975) is the first of a projected pair of minutely detailed volumes covering much of the same period. In addition, Kennedy now runs the Centre for Oral Traditions at Dartington, where his archives are available for study and research. Cassettes of selected artists and subjects are issued regularly, and provide an essential library of all the traditional musics of this country, including Welsh, Cornish, Channel Islands French and Manx Gaelic.

In spite of the musical success of *As I Roved Out*, it seemed almost as if the BBC was alone in its enthusiasm, as there was little apparent immediate effect. Two pioneering collections of songs appeared – A. L. Lloyd's *Come All Ye Bold Miners* (1952; new enlarged edition, Lawrence and Wishart, 1978) and Ewan MacColl's *The Shuttle and the Cage* (1954) – but little else of any relevance. It is significant that both of these collections were devoted to industrial songs, a direct result of the left-wing interests of both men, and a first indication of the hitherto untapped wealth of music both from the Industrial Revolution itself and from the post-Revolution period. Ewan MacColl, working on a project for the BBC, persuaded his producer to put advertisements in the railwaymen's journals and to write to loco sheds to ask if anyone knew songs. 'To our incredible surprise, within a day of the appeal appearing, we got things like "Poor Paddy Works on the Railway" . . . "Moses of the Mail" and half a dozen other pieces. And then we began to get songs from the iron foundries in Dundee, and it was obvious that nobody had really bothered to explore this area of our tradition. Bert [A. L. Lloyd], of course, had been conscious of it and had been collecting by post; he'd a great mass of material that went into *Come All Ye Bold Miners*, which is a magnificent collection. But the extraordinary thing is that nobody knew that this existed. People had taken it for granted that the only folk music was created out of the pastoral conditions, ignoring the fact that we had industries that went back to medieval times.'

There the matter rested briefly until the end of the fifties, when two more significant publications appeared. The first came in 1957 – V. S. de Sola Pinto's anthology of broadside and popular poetry entitled *The Common Muse*. Coming as it did at a time of considerable sensitivity towards possible obscenity, the publishers produced two editions, the more expensive one having an appendix of verses that might have led to actions for obscene libel at a more generally accessible price. To many the gutsiness and the naturalness of the language came as unexpected stimulation, and in the months to come the book became almost a secular bible for certain sectors of the folk world. And, apart from the printed sources, Pinto also dipped a toe into the oral tradition to print texts for such well-known epics as 'There Was a Monk of High Renown' and 'Harry Pollitt'.

More centrally, and therefore more importantly, the publication in 1959 of *The Penguin Book of English Folk Songs*, edited by Ralph Vaughan Williams and A. L. Lloyd, provided fledgling folksingers with just the source of songs that they needed, and at a price they could afford. Many of the songs spread like wildfire round the clubs and for a period at least those particular versions came almost to be accepted as *the* versions. Even now, in the late 1970s, the book retains its enormous prestige, and has been followed by other Penguin anthologies of songs from other countries.

By this time the Folk Revival was gathering momentum, and there was now an eager audience for new material. The work of Lloyd and MacColl had alerted other, younger collectors to the riches still to be mined. Nevertheless, the movement was still finding its feet, and much of the initial research was in libraries rather than in the field.

In 1960 Ewan MacColl and Peggy Seeger brought out their *Singing Island*, another seminal source book for young singers, but it was seven years before the first major analytical work appeared. In A. L. Lloyd's sweeping study *Folk Song in England* (1967) there came the first overall study of English song, both rural and industrial, together with the first attempts to relate it to the European tradition. (Frank Howes' *Folk Music of*

Britain and Beyond, published in 1969, pursued these relationships much further, at times to the point of extreme tenuousness.) Lloyd's book had an immense impact and remains, in spite of certain clear imbalances, the only authoritative general study yet published. At about the same time, Francis Collinson's *Traditional Music of Scotland* dealt with the same subject in the north, though from a considerably more musical and less sociological point of view.

On a much more rarified level, the American musicologist Professor Bertrand Bronson had spent the decade publishing the various volumes of his massive undertaking to restore the music to Child's *English and Scottish Popular Ballads*. *The Traditional Tunes of the Child Ballads*, which eventually comprised four hefty volumes, brought the best of American scholarship to a task which would have daunted many, and provided an enormous amount of rationalised material for a hungry Folk Revival. Unfortunately, Bronson has not yet been released in paperback, and the present hardback price of around £25 per volume drastically restricts its popular use.

If Bronson's work in collecting and collating thousands of examples of music is of almost epic proportions, his learned and often witty introductions are of equal importance, for they demonstrate that here is one professor at least who is aware of the practicalities of life. Bronson is only too aware that he is working in an electronic age and that folksong too exists in that framework. Further, if folksong exists in an electronic age, it must willy-nilly be affected by it. Specifically, the criterion of oral transmission of songs can no longer be a yardstick by which the traditionality of a song can be judged. Methods of transmission inevitably reflect the age in which they exist: in the days of general illiteracy, oral transmission must be the method by

22

which songs are learned; in a later age, when literacy is gaining ground, reading must be added to oral transmission as a valid means of learning, and broadsides (and, later, newspapers and songbooks) become acceptable. And in an age where communication is dominated by television, radio and hi-fi, then these methods of learning must surely be accepted with as good grace as possible.

As far back as 1907, the folklorist F. B. Gummere, while discussing the nature of traditional song, used the phrase '. . . whilst conditions of oral transmission may be changed'. He went on to say that, under such conditions, 'there is nothing to prevent the daily production of ballads which may become in time as popular as any in our collections'. Now, at that time, such a sentiment was truly revolutionary, and Gummere himself at length rejected it as a viable concept. Nonetheless, subsequent scholars have come more and more to accept Gummere's first tentative thought. Bronson himself, in his Introduction to Volume One of his work, writes: 'Subsequent opinion has inclined more and more to adopt Gummere's rejected alternative, that "while conditions of oral transmission may be changed" – *be it* via *cinema, television, radio or phonograph!* [my italics – FW] – "there is nothing to prevent the daily productions of ballads. . . ." And this, we may feel, is a view to which Child . . . might have become reconciled.'

And later on in the same section, Bronson writes: 'In the second quarter of the century, sound-recordings have tended to take over more and more of the burden of responsible preservation and transmission of evidence. . . . The right procedure for a future editor . . . will probably be to prepare a series of vocal recordings from authentic sources, and accompany them with critical and analytical notes, illustrated where desirable with selected passages transcribed for comparative study. It seems idle to reduce the living, truthful record with dogged persistence to a dim reflection, except where discussion may be facilitated.'

In Bronson's words we have, in fact, two quite separate implications. One is that, in this present society, it is permissible for a traditional singer to learn his repertoire by listening to gramophone records or a television programme; the other is a long-delayed vindication of Percy Grainger's once-despised beliefs.

To take the former statement, it must be admitted that, in fact, the thought is not really very startling. There is, after all, only a difference in degree between a traditional singer learning from a broadside and one learning from a record; and, indeed, one established traditional singer at least – Fred Jordan – sees nothing extraordinary in learning from records. Jordan was, for a time, in a position of especial pressure, in that for some years he was just about the only known English traditional singer who was available for and willing to appear at festivals. During this period he clearly felt that he had a responsibility to extend his repertoire and he did it in the most satisfactory way open to him. Nowadays, with many singers appearing at festivals and clubs all over the country, there is little sense of isolation and therefore less pressure to push back the accepted boundaries of learning.

Nevertheless, Bronson's statement does raise some fascinating side questions. Is a revivalist singer who learns his songs from the records of a traditional singer actually a traditional singer and not a revivalist? And, further and even more tangentially, is the child of a revivalist singer, who has learned the songs through hearing his or her parents sing them, a traditionalist or a revivalist? Clearly, there is a fair amount of rethinking to be done in terms of definitions, or the line between a 'traditional' traditionalist and a revivalist are going to

Charlie Wills: a great singer – and character

Above: (*left*) The East Anglian traditional singer Harry Cox, and (*right*) Fred Jordan, farmworker from Shropshire. *Below*: (*left*) the late Jeannie Robertson, the acknowledged Queen of traditional singers; and (*right*) Walter Pardon

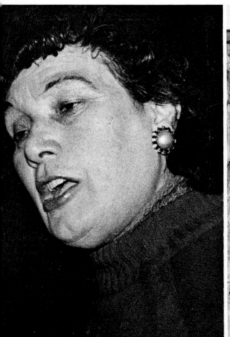

Shantyman Stan Hugill (*top left*), Scottish singer Jimmy McBeath (*top right*); and (*right*) The Copper family – from left to right Ron, John, Bob and Jill

Two of the Folk
Revival's cornerstones:
Ewan MacColl (*left*)
and Alex Campbell
(*below*)

Top: The original
Watersons: (left to right)
Norma, John Harrison,
Mike and Lal
Waterson. *Above*:
guitarist Davey Graham.
Right: An archetypal line-
up of Fairport Convention
(left to right) – Dave
Pegg, Dave Mattacks,
Dave Swarbrick, Simon
Nicol

Above : The Boys of the Lough : left to right Dave Richardson, Aly Bain, Cathal McConnell, Robin Morton. *Below* : two leading contemporary singer-songwriters Ralph McTell (*left*) and Harvey Andrews

Above: Bob Pegg (*left*) and Dick Gaughan
Below: Peter Bellamy (*left*) and Cyril Tawney during the recording of Bellamy's ballad-opera *The Transports*

Martin Carthy, the most influential of the second generation of revivalist singers

blur into uselessness. Already the accepted categories are largely meaningless in the case of some singers working within the Revival: Dick Gaughan, for instance, who learned much of his initial repertoire at home; or Aly Bain, to whom the traditional fiddler Tom Anderson has clearly stood *in loco parentis*; or Alex Campbell, whose long total absorption in the music surely now merits consideration in traditional terms. And contrariwise, many seem to consider Ewan MacColl a revivalist singer because he works within the Revival, whereas he is clearly traditional.

Further, the Norfolk singer Walter Pardon, only relatively recently discovered, has already used printed texts to complete lyrics that he only knew incompletely, in order to record his repertoire.

And, of course, while we're discussing this blurring of boundaries, we can hardly fail to consider the steadily-growing number of professionally-written songs that have already entered into the tradition. MacColl's 'Manchester Rambler' has been collected in British Columbia as a logging song ('I'm a logger, I'm a logger . . .') and songs by Dave Moran, John Conolly, Martin Graebe and others have been credited to 'Trad' on record labels – frustrating, no doubt, but a compliment in its way.

But, as with all things revolutionary, one must handle Bronson's statement carefully if it is not to get out of hand. On the surface, it would appear as if his approval of transmission by television or LP records endorses even rock music as folk – if not traditional folk, at least potentially traditional. The argument goes that (say) punk rock is popular, i.e. it is sung by the people, and is transmitted by a method approved by the folkloristic authorities; therefore punk rock is the folk music of the present and, presumably, the future.

But this is really a load of arrant trendy nonsense. You

might as well say that *all* music – with the possible exception of progressive jazz and the more appalling of the twentieth-century 'classical' composers – is folk music, using that bludgeoning technique, and applying only part of the range of criteria. The desire for making an attention-grabbing statement is here far stronger than its underlying logic, because any statement of this sort has not only to abide by the criteria, *it has to be self-evidently true*. If it is not self-evidently true, then the logic is false – as it is in this case. Apart from which, it renders all relevant definitions totally useless, and is therefore a sterling example of destructive posturing.

However, without all that sort of exaggerated nonsense, it must be accepted that the boundaries accepted by our Victorian and Edwardian forebears have been radically changed by post-war technological developments; though, in practical terms, the retention in their accepted senses of words like 'traditional' and 'revival' would be both sensible and appropriately down-to-earth.

Turning to the second of Bronson's points, it is now quite clear that a great deal of primary research is being done in terms of recordings rather than pen-and-ink. Whereas in earlier times a collector would publish a book of songs – of a region or of a singer – nowadays he will, more likely than not, release a commercial or semi-commercial gramophone record. Leaving aside a few earlier examples, the great explosion of records of traditional musicians began in the early 1970s, and is still increasing today, though the emphasis is now on instrumentalists.

Some are genuine archive recordings, such as the Leader Records LP of some of Grainger's 1908 cylinder recordings, including several songs from the renowned Joseph Taylor, and some derive from the later field-work of Peter Kennedy and the collectors of the School of Scottish Studies. Many, however, are studio recordings, with all the benefits of controlled conditions and superior equipment. The four-record set *A Song for Every Season* by the Copper family, the records of Fred Jordan, Walter Pardon, Lizzie Higgins and many more are precisely what Bronson was calling for, and – as Bronson also wished – they are in most cases backed up with a battery of background information and analysis.

But actual fieldwork still goes on. The work of Mike Yates in the south-east of England – and, in particular, among the gypsies – has set and maintained remarkable standards, as has the collecting of the Irishman Tom Munelly. Ewan MacColl's and Peggy Seeger's continuing work, particularly their in-depth study of the Stewart family, remains impeccable. In Scotland, Ireland and – at last – in Wales, the work of collecting and collating is still going on apace, demonstrating yet again that folk music is far from dead in these islands. Much of the work of the younger scholars is discussed elsewhere in this book; for the moment it is sufficient to note that the ubiquitous cassette recorder has made every man his own collector – often regardless of the legality of the recording. The sight of a veritable forest of microphones raised by the audience at any festival is strong indication of the continuing strength of the acquisitive instinct – even though, as I say, such recording is totally illegal. Folk fans who will rail at established collectors taking all the proceeds from songs they have collected, regardless of the moral claims of the original singers, rarely stop to think that they are doing the same thing themselves by depriving the singer of possible royalties from the sale of records. No one wishes to smother the desire to learn, but in another sphere, textbooks carry royalties for their authors, and it is to be hoped that future copyright legislation in Britain will eliminate some of the appalling anomalies present in the existing Act.

Such books as still appear fall into three categories: collections of songs by professional writers, usually those on the more commercial end of the folk spectrum, such as Ralph McTell or Harvey Andrews; run-of-the-mill collections of well-known songs (music publishers occasionally have the idea of putting together a bundle of arbitrarily chosen songs, loosely categorised as folk, but often containing some priceless howlers; these are intended to be cheap potboilers where the publishers do not have to pay royalties to composers); and a new category of anthology that I can only describe as 'creative anthologies'. In these the items are selected and juxtaposed with care, illustrated with contemporary pictures, and devoted to a purpose at once more complicated and useful than the mere supplying of works and music. They are, in fact, extremely imaginative teaching aids.

It will be seen, therefore, that most of the serious research work is being done in the field of recording. Books in the third category, such as those by Roy Palmer and Jon Raven, are constructive uses of base material, but remain essentially interpretative. It is rare nowadays for new song discoveries to be presented in printed form: 1977 saw the publication of two slim volumes of songs collected by Grainger, and 1978 brought an even slimmer volume of songs collected by George Butterworth, but little pioneering work is now done in book form, generally speaking. One cannot include the recent (1974) Oxford edition of *Cecil Sharp's Collection of English Folk Songs* edited by Maud Karpeles. In the first place, though a large publication – two fat volumes in a slipcase – it presented little that was new and, in scholarly terms, it was of little real significance. I was left inescapably with the cynical thought that the edition was prepared simply because the copyright on Sharp's collections expired in 1974: a new edition would effectively continue the copyright – and therefore the publisher's royalties – for another fifty years after the new editor's death. Oddly enough, a new edition of Baring-Gould appeared in the year *his* copyright expired, too!

So much for the work that has been done. Let us now turn to the subjects of that work – the traditional singers and musicians themselves.

The Singing Tradition

In the decade immediately following World War II there was only a mere handful of known traditional singers in Britain – known, that is, to the music world. All of them were elderly and had already been visited by collectors. As we have already seen, Harry Cox was discovered in 1921, but was then ignored until after the war; Charlie Wills' songs had been collected; that magnificently eccentric singer Sam Larner had given of his repertoire; Henry Burstow had poured out his songs also. But it was not until the early years of the Revival that the young people's attention began to turn back to the original song-carriers. Traditional singers, particularly Cox and Wills, became meccas for young singers, anxious to hear songs in their 'original' form. It was at this point that the function and role of the traditional singer began to change; or, more accurately, began to be changed for him.

In earlier generations, the singer was an essential part of a limited community, usually a village. His main auditorium was the village pub, and his audience his friends and fellow-villagers; a static, virtually unchanging audience which already knew the singer's repertoire probably by heart, but which nonetheless continued to draw entertainment from it. They also respected a singer's repertoire as a possession; no one would sing old Charlie's songs while Charlie was still capable of singing them himself – a primitive, but effective, form of copyright.

Further, respect for the singer's craft was total. As Bob Copper recalled in his superb book *A Song for Every Season*: 'When a singer was called upon for a song he was accorded the utmost attention and there was absolute silence until the whole company were invited to join in the chorus. Then a great wave of sound from a score of lusty throats would rise up and nearly burst the walls of the small room in an effort to ring out across the sky and tell the world that Sussex sheep-shearers could play just as hard as they could work. Their lives were the richer because of this.'

It must be emphasised here that the audience barely changed over the years: a few old faces would disappear and some new, fresh ones would take their place. But by and large the limitations of the audience were tight indeed, and this worked upon the singer in his turn. Possessed of a finite number of songs – though some singers were reputed to have had hundreds of songs in their heads – a singer had to hone his music to the finest point in his capacity if he was going to continue to hold attention. Not every singer could aspire to the highest ranks, naturally, but this factor alone goes a long way towards explaining the high percentage of very individual stylists among traditional singers, and the considerable number of singers who were and are capable of performances of a high artistic standard.

When the collectors and, later, the first of the young revivalist singers began to appear, the singer's role was immediately subtly changed. From being part of a community activity, he became a solo artist, separated (however slightly at this point) from his audience. He became someone to be deferred to, not someone to be accepted; he became, in a word, special. Few changed noticeably, of course; singers and collectors were welcomed into homes and pubs, and unstintingly given both hospitality and songs.

Unfortunately, in this process, the singers gave away not merely their songs, but also their age-old rights to the songs – as in a parallel way some primitive tribes still believe that to be photographed is to give away part of one's soul. For thanks to some disgraceful drafting in the 1911 Copyright Act – even more shamefully retained in the 1956 Act – all copyright in collected traditional music belongs to the collector who first 'fixes' (i.e. either writes down or records) the tune, or to the editor who may merely add a few phrase marks. Through ignorance on the part of the singer and, in many cases, the collector, singers were thus deprived of royalties on recordings and public performances to which they should have been entitled. Sadly, not too many people seem to have been very concerned about this, and the casualness with which this situation has been treated remains one of the few points of bad taste in the Folk Revival. The contrasting general resentment when Paul Simon used 'Strawberry Fair' from the singing of Martin Carthy without credit was quite remarkable; but then Martin Carthy is a much-respected and well-loved Revival singer, and not an obscure traditional singer known to few.

But, reverting to the changing position of traditional singers, if change did not come at once, it came within a relatively few years. As more traditional singers were found, and as folk festivals began to flourish, so the singers were invited as guest artists. And then, at one fell swoop, came the complete distortion of everything a traditional singer stands for. From singing in his own community, to a small audience, for love (or at the most for drinks), he began to sing to audiences of several hundreds, or even thousands, on a concert platform, for money. From being an amateur in his home surroundings, fulfilling a need of his friends, he became a 'star', a professional – or at least a semi-professional – in conditions as far removed as possible from the intimacy of his local pub.

There is no sneer in that remark about money; of course he *should* be paid in such circumstances. But the fact is that he has been pitchforked into an alien situation of relatively mass adulation and therefore forced to be false.

Now, it is possible to overstate this situation, and perhaps some of my readers will already have decided that I have done just that. To be sure, many traditional singers react with superb aplomb to their new position; but many, it is plain, feel ill at ease and strained. But the main point is not so much that the singers may or may not feel embarrassed; it is rather that folk music has been wrenched into a false context and will never be quite the same again.

In the preceding chapter I discussed the present interpretation of oral transmission, and how it has inevitably changed with improved methods of communication. From that, however, one can go even further and, in the light of the present situation of the traditional singer in Britain, say that the whole question of transmission is totally superfluous. If the Shropshire singer Fred Jordan can learn new songs from gramophone records, and if Harry Snooks can learn songs direct from Walter Pardon via an illicit cassette or even a legal LP, then where is the point of making any distinction at all? Folk music is no longer a thing of the villages and local pubs – only a few in England now have this kind of music since the majority have opted for the canned variety – it has become a thing of concert platforms, tours and commercial recordings. The function of a traditional singer is no longer to hold and transmit a core of songs in his own community, but to broadcast them at large, to strangers. Folksingers no longer represent a manifestation of village life, but a small segment of show-business.

To say this – to lament it, even – is not necessarily to condemn the present situation. Clocks must move forward, after all, and what is, *is*. But in future folksong will have to be studied in this light, and not in its original and proper relation to a small community. Whether the change is for good or ill, who can say at this juncture? In one sense, it is all to the good, as the songs are disseminated to a far wider audience and will therefore remain alive that much more easily; in another sense it is to the bad, since folk music has, like it or not, lost its essential intimacy. One can say either that it has come of age, or that it has been deflowered, according to one's own view; but if the Folk Revival has had any major effect on the traditional music of these islands, it is surely that it has put traditional music irrevocably off course. I doubt if anyone would be so arrogant as to attempt to prophesy its future.

If the foregoing strikes as unduly pessimistic – and it is meant to be questioning rather than anything else – we can at least take comfort in the numbers of traditional singers now available to audiences. As I have said, the early fifties knew only a handful of singers. We are now blessed with what could almost be called an abundance, with new singers being discovered at gratifyingly frequent intervals. How long this can last is anybody's guess, but the last few years have thrown up Walter Pardon, Johnny Doughty and Frank Hinchcliffe, all in their way discoveries of pure gold. The more established singers have been sedulously cherished, recorded and interviewed, and there is more raw material available for study at this present time than ever before.

In England, the oldest generation of singers finally disappeared at the beginning of the 1970s, with the deaths of Harry Cox and Charlie Wills. Sam Larner,

George 'Pops' Maynard and others had already died, together with many lesser lights. But with the departure of those folk giants, other new names began to emerge as amateur and professional collecting proliferated. First and foremost, the Copper family strode from obscurity to become the indisputable leaders among the ranks of traditional singers. Known as a singing family in and around Rottingdean for over two hundred years, their part-singing came as a revelation to an audience accustomed only to solo performers. The Revival groups The Young Tradition and The Watersons led the way in emulating their characteristic style, and the Copper style is still to be heard in practically every revivalist group with more than two participants – and even in quite a few with only two.

In 1971 they recorded a four-record set *A Song for Every Season*, matched by Bob Copper's prize-winning book of the same title; the recordings were a revealing and fascinating blend of the family's music and their reminiscences – reminiscences of old country ways, family occasions, festivals and work, which introduced the songs and brought them alive in a way no purely musical presentation could ever have achieved. The death of Bob's cousin Ron, in early 1978, has reduced the group to a trio, but a future generation will be brought up in the family traditions and hopefully the Coppers will still be singing in Sussex in another two hundred years.

Fred Jordan, a Shropshire farmworker who learned his basic repertoire from his family, other farmworkers and passing gypsies, has been the most closely adopted by the folk world, especially the folk 'establishment' that centres round the English Folk Dance and Song Society. Jordan, who is somewhere in his fifties – he himself gives varying answers to questions about his birth – has come to be completely at home with concert and club audiences. Indeed, he positively flowers when faced with a large audience whom he can turn and tease with a totally deadpan humour which at first is not always wholly obvious. His singing, too, contains subtleties which are not immediately apparent; it is only after several hearings that his artfulness, his considerable sense of drama and structure, begin to emerge.

Stan Hugill comes from an older generation (though this is rarely apparent) and claims to have been the last professional shantyman in the days of sail. A colleague of mine once used the gargantuan phrase 'autodidactic polymath' to describe Thomas Hardy; the phrase fits Hugill equally well. A superb and hypnotic talker and a bluff singer of enormous energy, he has produced several standard works on sea songs of all kinds and, as our one remaining link with maritime songs of work and leisure, is clearly one of the key figures not only in the Revival but in the modern history of traditional song.

Walter Pardon was discovered in 1973 by the young singer Peter Bellamy, who not only launched him with great success but also protected his interests with exemplary consideration. Pardon had learned most of his songs from his father and uncle, but had never sung in public at all until the mid-seventies; during the intervening years he had sung merely to himself, keeping his considerable repertoire alive in his mind. He has already made two recordings and many festival appearances, and his repertoire has proved to contain both hitherto unknown songs and hitherto unknown variants.

Johnny Doughty, an even more recent discovery, made his recording début – like fledgling pop stars, traditional singers now tend to make their first appearances on record – in 1976. A retired fisherman from

Rye, Doughty also has a strong repertoire which he presents with such relishing aplomb that he sometimes seems to have spent a lifetime on the halls.

Sussex generally has proved to be rich in traditional singers, all of whom are still active. Folk audiences are well familiar not merely with the Coppers and Doughty, but also with George Spicer, Bob Blake, George Belton, Cyril Phillips, Ernest 'Rabbidy' Baxter, Mary Ann Haynes, Bob Lewis and Harry Upton, all of whom have also made or taken part in commercial recordings.

East Anglia, too, has provided a gratifying number of singers, partly centred round two pubs where folk-singing in the traditional sense still goes on – The Ship and The Eel's Foot at Blaxhall. Bob Hart is one such, as was Percy Webb, who died in 1977; Ernest Austin comes from Essex; the bargeman Bob Roberts, though Dorset-born, has spent all his life in Suffolk; and Walter Pardon is a Norfolk man.

The West Country, as might be expected in an area where traditional music has always been strong, has also been rich in singers and musicians; notably, in recent years, Bob Cann, Charlie Bate and Mervyn Kitchen.

Northwards, the situation is less impressive, though the recent appearance of the Yorkshire singer Frank Hinchcliffe has redressed the balance to some degree. There is, of course, an extremely lively north-eastern tradition, but this is mainly instrumental and is discussed elsewhere.

It is significant that in England we tend to consider ourselves fortunate in this respect, for in Scotland and Ireland an even stronger situation is taken virtually for granted. Both countries have areas that are more remote than anywhere in England, and in such areas particularly the traditions have not needed to be 'revived' as they have never really ceased to be a part of ordinary life. In Ireland especially the musical pub is a commonplace, and few folk clubs, in the English sense, are needed for the nurturing of traditional music.

It is self-evident that the further away from so-called civilisation a place is, the more likely it will be that old customs and traditions will continue naturally and unselfconsciously. To an extent this explains the richness of the present East Anglian situation (though I must confess it does not help to explain that of Sussex); and the Highlands and Islands of Scotland bear eloquent testimony to the correlation. The tape archives of the School of Scottish Studies (slowly, but magnificently, being released by Tangent Records) and the written documentation being published in the School's two journals, show a remarkable wealth still continuing vitally in the Gaelic tradition. Bards and singers, story-tellers and instrumentalists appear with ever-increasing frequency the further north-west one travels.

With the exception of people like the late Calum Ruadh, whose bardic functions made his work essentially public, most of the singers and musicians are *family* performers only. Singers like Murdina MacDonald, Mrs Archie MacDonald and Mary Morrison are closer, in function and attitude, to those of the early traditional singer than are the Scottish and Lowland Scots traditional singers, accustomed as the latter are to relatively frequent appearances in a concert situation.

But understandably enough these singers are barely known to the Folk Revival, which is essentially English orientated. Rare indeed, even in Scotland, are the festival appearances of Gaelic-speaking singers; only Flora McNeil is at all known in a general sense, as a result of some tours with the Boys of the Lough. Is it cynical to observe that perhaps this is as it should be? At least the music and its functions have not been distorted by being wrenched into a selfconscious context. At any rate, the Gaelic tradition is, if not flourishing, at least continuing on its way – though a gradual decline must inevitably be tied to the overall diminution in the speaking of the language.

Of all the recent Scottish traditional singers, the name of Jeannie Robertson must come first in any consideration. Possessed of a superb repertoire of ballads and songs, and with a voice of power and purity such as has been given to few other folksingers, Jeannie Robertson dominated the Scottish – if not the European – folk scene until her death in 1975. She received an MBE for her services to music, a unique honour for a singer.

Her daughter, Lizzie Higgins, now carries the mantle, together with the related family of travellers, the Stewarts of Blair: Sheila, Belle, Alex, Cathie, Davie, Lucy, Jane, Christina and Sheila.

But apart from the enormous wealth of the Stewart–Higgins lineage, Scotland can offer many other fine traditional singers. The late Jimmy MacBeath, a man with a face like a tortured relief-map, sang songs from the north-east of Scotland, always one of the most fertile areas for song in the British Isles. John McDonald, 'the singing molecatcher', the Border shepherd Willie Scott, Isabel Sutherland, John Strachan, Jane and Cameron Turriff, Dave and Betty Campbell – these and many more have provided a broad sweep of songs and styles, both in live performance and on record. All of them are or have been also active participants in the Folk Revival, as well as singing in their own environment. Further, there are the leading figures of Ewan MacColl and Jean Redpath, both traditional singers, but working exclusively in the Revival framework and usually considered as revivalist singers; the categorisation is wrong, but both are discussed, for convenience, in the section on the Revival.

These, as I have already remarked, are the singers whom the Revival knows; but there are dozens of others known mainly to the field-workers and researchers, and whose contributions are published in *Tocher*, a magazine published three times a year by the School of Scottish Studies. And perhaps this is as it should be. It is good – indeed, essential – to have the chance to hear traditional singers; but it is also essential to have at least some small part of the tradition continuing to exist in its proper milieu, natural and true to itself.

The same situation obtains in Ireland, where conditions are not dissimilar to those in Scotland. There is a strong nucleus of 'star' singers, known through recordings and public appearances, backed up by many known only in their village or area.

The scene has been probably dominated by two families, the Tunneys and the Makems. The singing of both Brigid Tunney and her son Paddy demonstrates the mastery of that lyrical, ornamented style that seems to flourish in Ireland. Sarah Makem and her mother, together with her son Tommy have all been outstanding singers in their varied way, the youngest member of the family having shown that he remained a fine solo singer in spite of many years of singing with the Clancy Brothers.

Joe Heaney emigrated to America in the early 1960s and has remained there, establishing himself among the Irish population of New York – and, through records, with the British as well – as a rare stylist and singer of great strength. Packie Byrne, too, is an emigré, having lived in London now for many years. Both as whistler and singer, he has long been one of the leading traditional figures working virtually entirely within the Revival. In his recent partnership with the young Canadian singer and harpist Bonnie Shaljean, he has created not only an attractive dual act but also an intriguing amalgam of styles and traditions.

One more singer should be mentioned, if only as an indication of the 'unknown' stratum of Irish traditional singing. John Maguire is a small farmer in County Fermanagh. Although he has made an LP, he appears but rarely at folk festivals and continues to farm his smallholding. Judged by the repertoire revealed by his record and by the book about him (*Come Day, Go Day, God Send Sunday*, Routledge, 1973) he is without question a singer who could, if he chose, rank with the more public figures of the Irish tradition. As in Scotland, many traditional singers prefer to go their own way and avoid the limelight. We can only reckon ourselves fortunate that they at least agree to record.

I have said nothing so far of Wales, for the simple reason that very little is known in the world at large. Folk music is sung in the hills, and a great deal of it has been recorded by the Welsh Folk Museum. So far only two records have been issued, and those so recently that they have not had time to percolate.

Traditional song in Welsh is, of course, like Gaelic, limited in its appeal by the language barrier, and only two revivalist groups have so far tried to introduce such material into their acts.

There is a strong feeling that the Nonconformist church did much to destroy the Welsh tradition, and certainly the dominance of the male voice choir would seem to uphold this theory. How far the music actually is dead, though, seems increasingly open to doubt, and future releases from the Folk Museum's archives may well force a basic reassessment.

Among the English-speaking Welsh traditional singers, the name of Phil Tanner stands supreme. It is said that he was possessed of 'an inexhaustible repertoire', and his warm, feeling voice and dramatic sensitivity would have made him a major singer in any country. Sadly, Tanner appears to be one of the few leading traditional singers of the postwar era not currently represented in the record catalogues.

These Isles – and England in particular – have always enjoyed (if that is the correct word) the reputation of being unmusical. Dr Burney observed that the only folk music we possessed were the hornpipe and the Cheshire Round, and even in the late nineteenth and early twentieth centuries the same charges were levelled by continental critics.

The Victorian collectors answered those charges in round terms, but nonetheless pessimistically misread the signs. The passage of time and further research – conducted to more exacting standards and over a wider, deeper field – have demonstrated that, so far from being the moribund tail-end of a once-lively tradition, British national music is still wagging with fairly brisk health. If traditional song and singers have been absorbed – more than a touch artificially – into the Folk Revival, then the singers in question have adapted themselves to new circumstances. Uprooted from the fireside of a local pub on to a concert platform, they have largely met the challenge with a *sang-froid* that is wholly British. Given that modes of transmission have changed, and given that the class of participants has also changed, one cannot help thinking that the folk tradition is in a healthier state now than it has been for a long time – and certainly so if one judges health by width of dissemination. Traditional song might never be quite the same again, but it is certainly sung by and heard by many, many more people than ever before. And even if the tradition itself dies out – which history would seem to deny – the songs themselves seem assured of a continuing, if separate, existence.

The Instrumental Tradition

As the singing tradition was surviving in its own quiet way, so the instrumental tradition also sustained itself between the wars and beyond. In this period, the musicians were largely tied to and supported by the social dance. Instrumental ensembles did not exist mainly for concert work as many do now and, indeed, the whole concept of any kind of concert was and is alien to traditional music. To an extent also, the ritual dance kept alive a certain number of instrumentalists, though this was necessarily limited both in numbers and types.

In Scotland the music centred around the pipes and the fiddle. In the far north, Tom Anderson and his family were providing music for dances and preserving the individual music of the Shetlanders, later to be passed on to the outstanding young revivalist fiddler Aly Bain. The massed strings of Anderson's unique orchestra Ra Forty Fiddlers were also available for dances on a more spectacular scale, and still are.

Further south, fiddlers such as Scott Skinner and Hector McAndrew perpetuated and continually added to a huge repertoire of dancing and listening tunes, honing and refining a tradition already glowing from the hands of predecessors such as Neil Gow. It was their task to provide music for the local dances and ceilidhs and both the music and the style of playing are largely geared to this function. The Celtic countries, though, also listened between the dances, and the national repertoires contain a wealth of haunting airs. Oddly, none seems to exist in England, where all the music is functional.

The pipers provided the more ceremonial music;

indeed, the classic repertoire of the Highland pipes contains no dances at all, and it is only later philosophies and breakaways that have added the 'lower' type of music. The great pipes were originally war instruments, and remained either martial or threnodic until the development of the chamber pipes.

Nowadays pipers tend to stem from military or quasi-military training and thus appear to stand outside the Folk Revival – as do, indeed, the traditional fiddlers. In both cases, however, the reverse is true, in that it is actually the Revival that is standing outside a valid and living tradition, preferring to bring in its own instrumentalists for its various social occasions. It is true that there are few of the old fiddlers left now, and that the best, like Aly Bain and Tom Hickland, are revivalists; but it is nonetheless an unusual and rather sad situation. Traditional musicians are invited to Scottish festivals, as they are in England, but these are occasions which fail to approach them in their natural habitat, but rather wrench them into a revivalist context.

In Ireland, as evidenced by a recent plethora of recordings, the situation is extremely healthy. Every month, it seems, new traditional instrumentalists are being discovered and taped, mostly in the remoter parts of the island. Concertina-players, fiddlers and whistle-players predominate in this wealth of recorded material which is in the course of providing future generations with an impressive research archive. The musical standards are not uniformly high, but the impression of bustling life is unmistakable. Of these many musicians, one should mention especially the names of Packie Byrne, Jackie Daly, Johnny O'Leary, Rose Murphy, the Cliffords, Tommy Peoples and John Doonan.

The uillean pipes, being a considerably more difficult instrument to master, has few proponents. The late Leo Rowsome and his similarly-named son and, to a lesser extent, the late Felix Doran, together with Seamus Ennis, have long led the field, but it is difficult to define future generations that one could call traditional – if, indeed, pipers are ever traditional in the accepted sense, for the lengthy formal training essential for the achievement of any high musical and technical standards virtually takes the piper into the realms of classical training. Younger musicians like Paddy Moloney and Tomas O Canainn fall oddly between the stools in terms of definition; both have academic overtones which are perhaps inescapable nowadays in terms of such a complex instrument.

In England, the fiddle, the concertina and the melodeon have been kept alive through their association with the ritual dance, though a few instrumentalists, such as Scan Tester, remained separate and concentrated on providing entertainment music. William Kimber, who died in 1961, was an outstanding concertina-player with Headington Morris, and William 'Jinky' Wells performed a similar function on his fiddle for Bampton Morris. Each team had its own musicians, but the reputation of these two remains, thanks largely to their association with Cecil Sharp. To a large extent, however, this tradition was broken by World War I, and the Morris teams that dance nowadays are all revivals, though both Headington and Bampton claim an unbroken line. Musicians like Kimber and Wells, therefore, are rare in the field of dance music, and none exists today who approaches their stature as repositories of traditional music.

In the north-east of England, though, there was a more flourishing tradition, particularly where the Northumbrian small pipes were concerned. Here outstanding musicians such as Billy Pigg and Jack

Armstrong were not merely preserving an existing tradition, but actively adding to it almost daily. Pigg in particular wrote a host of pipe tunes of all kinds that are now eagerly snapped up by young revivalists.

Because of the concentration on the dance itself, both during the days of Sharp and now, the instrumental side has tended to be overlooked as far as recordings are concerned. While there are commercial recordings available of many singers, as far back as the 1908 recordings of Joseph Taylor, we have little or nothing in the way of English instrumental music played by traditional musicians. There is a little of Scan Tester available, a little of Kimber, nothing of Wells, and precious little of anyone else.

Scottish fiddlers such as Scott Skinner and Hector McAndrew are now available on LP, their early 78 rpm records – clear evidence of popular interest – having been reprocessed and enhanced; and pipe music is recorded fairly regularly, largely for the transatlantic expatriate audience. And as far as Shetland is concerned, thanks to Tom Anderson's involvement with the Revival through Aly Bain, several recordings are available – more, in fact, than are available of English traditional music. Ireland, as we have seen, is still a collector's paradise, with small record labels springing up to concentrate on national folk music.

But, as instrumental music in England is largely subservient to other requirements, it has tended to be somewhat of a Cinderella in terms of research and collecting. With the exception of a few who have achieved national status – and mostly discovered since the start of the Revival – most musicians have merely laboured in their own areas, content with a purely local reputation. There have been few instrumentalist stars in traditional music compared to the sphere of song.

Part 2
The Revival

The Song Revival

The 1950s were a watershed in more ways than one for the music industry. From entertainment delivered from a distance by a frankly older generation to adoring teenagers, it became a sharing between young people. The distance between star and fan was no less – indeed, it was often considerably greater, in the physical sense, as hysteria took over and the bodyguards moved in – but it was at least on some sort of ostensible level. The charts in the first half of the decade were dominated by singers such as Guy Mitchell, Frankie Laine and Dean Martin, though the first stirrings of rock 'n' roll were visible in the emergence of Bill Haley. The second half was notable for the solid weight of the new young stars: Presley, Jerry Lee Lewis, Tommy Steele, the Everly Brothers, Cliff Richard and Adam Faith.

This emphasis on youth was the first – and at that time totally unrecognised – hint of trouble for the old-fashioned music publishers. From now on the record companies would take over, making the hits and the money through control of publishing companies. In time, the stars themselves would form their own publishing companies, and the established publishers would be lucky if they got a token fee for accounting services.

In some ways, music publishers have still not come to terms with the new regime. Publishing (i.e. actually printing music) in the pop world is virtually non-existent compared to what it was in the thirties and, though publishers profit considerably from having hits, they actually do little to deserve it. Promotion and exploitation are controlled by the record companies, the investment is made by record companies, and success is related solely to record sales. The pop publishers' role has diminished to that of royalty collector, and it could be said that they only cling to this function by virtue of the fact that membership of the Performing Right Society and Mechanical Copyright Protection Society is, in this respect, limited to publishers.

This position first became apparent in the fifties, then, when the youngsters started to take matters into their own hands. Tired of being offered a tasteless diet of musical pap sung in an old-fashioned way by singers old enough to be their fathers, they looked for music that was more meaningful to them – music for themselves, of themselves and by themselves. And they found it initially, oddly enough, in the person of a professional jazz guitarist and banjoist, Lonnie Donegan, then playing in the Ken Colyer Jazz Band.

Skiffle had been played in Britain as far back as 1947, by a group called The Original London Blue Blowers. Colyer's interest was sparked to the extent that he went to New Orleans to learn it at source, returning to join Chris Barber and Monty Sunshine for a while before forming another band for himself. This band had an integral skiffle group which provided music during the official intervals. The group – the first British group to play skiffle professionally – comprised Colyer and Donegan on guitars, Bill Colyer on washboard and either Chris Barber or Jim Bray on bass.

That particular band didn't last long, however, and in 1953 Barber left to form his own band, taking with him the entire rhythm section, including Donegan. As with the Colyer band, skiffle became an established feature of the repertoire, and in 1954 there was a Donegan skiffle version of 'Rock Island Line' on one of the Barber LPs. Two years later it was released as a tentative single by Decca, and by the end of the first week in 1956 it had entered the charts, staying there for seventeen weeks, and reaching number six.

After that, Donegan went from strength to strength. In 1956 he had five records in the charts, though nothing reached the top, according to the *Record Retailer* listings. In 1957 another five appeared, with two number ones among them – 'Cumberland Gap' and 'Puttin' On the Style'. In 1958, the impetus had died. Three records reached the charts ('Tom Dooley' went to number three), but by 1959 Donegan had turned to non-skiffle masterpieces like 'Does Your Chewing-gum Lose Its Flavour on the Bedpost Overnight' and 'My Old Man's a Dustman' – big hits both of them, but nothing to do with skiffle.

The skiffle period was roughly the years 1956 and 1957. There were mutterings beforehand, and dying throes afterwards, but those two years saw the rise and fall of the craze. Oddly, in spite of the interest of Tin Pan Alley, and in spite of what has been said since, skiffle made little impact on the charts. Apart from Donegan, only two other acts achieved chart status: Chas McDevitt and Nancy Whiskey with 'Freight Train' and The Vipers with three singles in 1957, none of which went higher than eight.

Far more powerful than this commercially-orientated skiffle was the club scene, where the music was played in cellars and coffee bars throughout the land on a variety of instruments including tea-chest basses and washboards. The musical quality was not, by my memory, particularly high, but it was new, it was refreshing and – above all – it was enthusiastic, and it was a welcome gale of fresh air after the plastic performances of the crooners.

And it was certainly widespread. John Bird, in his book on skiffle, recalled that both the All-Scotland skiffle championship of 1957 and the East Anglian championship of 1958 attracted over a hundred groups. In a skiffle competition in the London area alone, between thirty and forty groups entered. Clubs sprang up all over the country, and groups proliferated, even down to the pre-teenage level. The attractions were obvious: it was cheap to get a band together, the music was gutsy, strongly rhythmic and intentionally rough, so that the odd wrong chord was hardly crucial. And it had an excitement about it that was *new*, as well as offering an opportunity to perform instead of being performed at. And, of course, there was – in theory at least – the possibility of discovery and stardom, though I doubt if that motive loomed very large in many minds at that time.

Understandably, in view of the American domination of entertainment, the repertoire was initially transatlantic, and derived from songwriters such as Leadbelly, Big Bill Broonzy, Uncle Dave Macon and Woody Guthrie, and American folksongs. These last were popularised by artists no longer generally identified with folk music, though – in the terms that existed then – some at least were genuinely involved and contributed a discernible impetus to the fledgling British scene. Most prominent among them was Burl Ives, as near to a traditional folksinger as an American star can get, having learned his songs on his father's farm and on the road from hobos, convicts and passing acquaintances. As his film career prospered, so his singing became less frequent and his image was corrupted (in folk terms, that is) by a succession of mawkish songs such as 'Itty-bitty Tear'. Nevertheless, though now into his seventies, he is still capable of singing superbly, even such technically demanding songs as 'Venezuela'.

Two other actors were, at that time, closely involved with folksinging: Harry Belafonte and Theodore Bikel, who topped many bills in the early fifties before another fame called them away.

But most of the emphasis was in the groups. These

54

flourished in the States at this time, and were largely concerned with souping-up otherwise innocuous folk-songs to the point where they were approachable by the general public. Of these the biggest commercial success was gained by The Kingston Trio and Peter, Paul and Mary. These two, being the most recorded and the most imported by Britain, were the main sources of inspiration to the up-and-coming revivalist singers; they were also directly responsible for the sudden rash of the hearty chorus-prone groups such as The Clancy Brothers and The Corries.

But other groups played their part too: The Almanac Singers, The Gateway Singers, The Rooftop Singers, The Weavers and – best of all – The Limeliters.

In a relatively short time, the trend faded away, as trends do (though Peter, Paul and Mary soldiered on until personal problems led to their break-up in the late sixties). Their work generally was extremely enter-taining and undeniably they turned many thousands of people on to the enjoyment of folksong. But their ar-rangements and their approach were also essentially soft-centred; they all–with the possible exception of The Limeliters – had that touch of saccharine so often found in American entertainment of that time. Their influence has now gone, but they had an enormous impact on British popular musical taste.

It was at this point that two superficially disparate elements met – with remarkable results.

At the beginning of the fifties, Ewan MacColl, already an established actor, singer and songwriter, was approached by the BBC to prepare a series of eight documentaries using folksong. In a 1973 interview with the present writer, he recalled: 'we themed the eight programmes: we did one on love, one on work, one on the brutal city, one on the sea, and all the rest of it. The sea one was the one that really broke through.

'At that time, the only singers we could really draw upon, that could handle scripted material, were Bert [Lloyd] and myself and Isla Cameron, and that was about it on the English side. On the American side we brought in Jean Ritchie, Big Bill Broonzy, [Alan] Lomax himself and the one or two other American traditional singers who were known and who happened to be in England or Europe at the time. When we did the sea one we scooped the pool because they'd never heard shanties sung in anything other than the way they were sung at school. Things like "Blood Red Roses" were done for the first time, and they had a shattering effect.'

Later MacColl moved into the concert field, putting on a series in the East End of London featuring himself, A. L. Lloyd, Alan Lomax, Fitzroy Coleman and the calypsonian Lord Kitchener.

'Now this was really the beginning of the folk revival, because the skiffle was getting going at the same time. I'm not saying it was all because of that, don't misunderstand me, that was merely a factor, an important factor. There were other factors, particularly the BBC things. People had had a pretty grey existence right through the years of the war, particularly young people, whether they'd been in the army or whether they'd not. It was a pretty dreary kind of life with all those old, old hackneyed numbers coming out of the sausage machine; you know, "Mexico Bay" and all those bloody things that went right through the war. People were fed up to the teeth with them. And to some extent it was an instinct of turning away from the media on the part of great masses of young people; not only in terms of music, but in terms of the development of theatre during this period, the development of film societies, the jazz movement, all these things were going on. Very exciting period.'

Before the skiffle movement had got under way, though, Ewan MacColl's first folk club had been established at the Princess Louise in High Holborn with a list of residents that included MacColl, Lloyd, Seamus Ennis and Fitzroy Coleman. And it was at this time also that MacColl's thinking took a major step forward. For the majority of his life he had been closely involved with popular (i.e. the people's) culture: street theatre, point songs, writing, producing all kinds of propaganda art-forms. But if this came from a Communist and therefore pan-national stimulus, MacColl's thinking at the Princess Louise became entirely national in that he decried the then British singers' habit of singing American (or Greek, or Israeli) songs, and insisted that an Englishman should sing English songs, an American American songs, a Scot Scottish songs, and so forth. And this insistence on the excellence and range of British folksong caught the skiffle singers and audience at the moment when they were looking for different repertoire. A worried man can go on singing a worried song only so long, and by the end of 1957 altogether too many bales of cotton had been picked. The British native folk repertoire was embraced with enthusiasm and vigour, and the Folk Revival was under way.

That, of course, is a considerable over-simplification. Strands had been in existence for some time, and others were to be added later – but if one has to date the beginning of the Revival then the middle fifties, and 1957 in particular, will do as well as any.

At that time, there was a substantial element of unaccompanied singing, though the guitar carried over from skiffle and became the overwhelmingly dominant

57

instrument, whatever lack of justification there may be for its inclusion in a British tradition. They are cheap, portable, and the minimum three chords can be learned quickly (alas, I sometimes think), so if nothing else they are eminently convenient.

For some time the Folk Revival stayed small and purist. There was only a handful of professional singers and there were precious few clubs for them to sing in. As Louis Killen recalled, 'When I started Folk Song and Ballad in Newcastle in 1958 there weren't twenty folk clubs in the whole country, and when I left for the States [in 1966] there were maybe three hundred.' At the time of writing there are probably around 1700.

Nevertheless, even with so few venues, there was a living to be made, albeit a frugal one, with fees around the £5 mark. But in those days there was an evangelising spirit which more than compensated for the lack of earning power.

As Killen has indicated, the proliferation of clubs was marked in those first few years, and the first generation of singers was, if few in number, sufficiently high in quality to keep the excitement on the boil. Most of them are now, if not quite legends, at least highly respected as elder statesman and models. Killen himself must be considered the foremost stylist of the time, and recent recordings and visits to Britain have confirmed that the intervening years have merely added maturity to an already striking range and depth of interpretation. Cyril Tawney and Harry Boardman also remain as active participants from those days, as does the archetypal Alex Campbell, now so completely imbued with traditional music that he can really be considered as a traditional rather than a revival singer. Shirley Collins, too, continues to sing, though her career in recent years has not embraced the endless series of one-night stands that is the normal lot of the professional singer.

And, of course, there is the giant figure of MacColl himself, still an active participant in everything from club gigs to field research, arguably the greatest and most dramatic singer, arguably the best songwriter in the field, indisputably the greatest teacher. He has had commercial success (his song 'The First Time Ever I Saw Your Face' was recorded by both Roberta Flack and Elvis Presley in 1972; the song secured a Novello Award) and – such is the nature of the folk world – the usual mud has been slung, as it is slung at anyone from the folk world who noticeably makes money. But such accusations rarely come from fellow singers, and arise from the intense possessiveness felt by audiences towards 'their' singers. The singers can sing pop songs, even rock 'n' roll, provided they sing them in the folk clubs; but they are liable to get bruised if they achieve success outside the clubs.

Far more singers have retired from the scene for one reason or another. Rory McEwen is now a successful professional painter, Stan Kelly (writer of, *inter alia*, 'Liverpool Lullaby') is now a computer consultant, Owen Hands runs a shop in Edinburgh, Enoch Kent is an advertising consultant in Canada. Sadly, their names are now scarcely known to the younger members of the folk audience.

In the group scene, a similar situation obtains. The Clancy Brothers, high priests of the stomping chorus song and fashion leaders in the field of Arran sweaters, have long lost their initial impetus and now confine their work to a few American concerts per year; in any case the original personnel is long gone, and lesser relations have taken the place of the first-generation Clancys. The Dubliners now attract a largely non-folk audience and have barely changed their act over the last ten years – a comment that can also be applied with fair accuracy to their Scottish counterpart The Corries. Both have, in fact, moved into the world of show-business and can now be considered not so much as folk artists as general entertainers using folk material.

The same description can be applied to The Spinners, whose price for *their* success has been rejection by the young folk audience, who know little about their continuing work behind the scenes on behalf of folk music and musicians.

The other early group, The Ian Campbell Folk Group, is now also in decline, largely owing in my opinion to an apparent inability or reluctance to find a new approach for the seventies. Styles and standards *have* changed and while folksong is not afflicted by fashion to any noticeable degree, development is inescapable. Nevertheless, both Lorna and Ian Campbell remain fine individual singers.

One must in all fairness make clear, though, that these groups undeniably brought thousands of young people to folk music in the earlier stages of the Revival, and were largely instrumental in creating the folk audience as it exists today.

The first few years of the Revival, then, were marked by a few outstanding solo artists, together with a variety of groups whose main common denominator was ruggedness rather than subtlety. These provided an element of audience participation and stimulation (the folderol syndrome) that was probably essential at that time if a new audience was going to be held. Had they remained at this average level, however, it is doubtful that much else would have happened. But by the middle of the sixties, a new generation – and kind – of singer was beginning to emerge. Instrumentally more proficient, considerably more sophisticated in terms of vocal technique (sometimes, inevitably, to a point approaching mannerism), they worked initially at one remove from the tradition. Coming as they did from largely middle-class homes without a tradition of music-making or the handing-on of songs, they were forced to learn their songs from the few records that were available, from occasional radio programmes, from songbooks and from each other. Many of them were also post-graduates or teachers, singing for a livelihood, but still supported by the existence of a qualification to fall back on. And to an extent this caused an immediate self-contradiction. For how could an educated, middle-class town-dweller possibly sing working-class rural songs with either understanding or conviction? At the time this argument – and other similar controversies – generated a fair amount of heat, but it is now, thank heavens, accepted that they can and do. And indeed, if it had not been for this influx of new blood it is doubtful whether the Revival could have survived. To get off the ground on a national basis, the movement needed sufficient competent singers to cover the country; and these could not have come from the first generation, nor (even more certainly) from the ranks of the genuine traditional singers, very few of whom were known at that time, and even fewer capable of travelling.

So, during the first seven or so years of the sixties, there emerged a group of singers who still dominate the club scene not only in their own right, but also as influential models. Because they are closer in age to both the younger audience and the rising third generation of singers, their effect is greater than that of the remaining first generation. Few young singers now attempt to sing like Ewan MacColl or Louis Killen; too many try to sing like Martin Carthy or Nic Jones.

Martin Carthy is quite clearly the most influential

singer to have emerged so far. He is both blessed and cursed with a markedly individual style of singing and playing. The angular, percussive style he has developed for his guitar is now almost synonymous with English folk guitar playing, together with the prevalence of open tunings which he originally developed in this field. In so far as his instrumental work has stimulated other and younger musicians this is all to the good; what is perhaps not so beneficial is that the other aspects of the guitar's tonal potential have tended to be ignored.

Carthy himself is a noticeably flexible musician, having worked solo, in an unaccompanied group (The Watersons) and in two electric bands (Steeleye Span in two phases, and The Albion Dance Band). He is at his best, however, in a solo context, when he can give himself room to bring out a song's full force. His lengthy, but cumulatively powerful, performances of 'Famous Flower of Serving Men' are a case in point.

The tag of 'superstar' has been hung around Carthy's neck so many times now that it is scarcely surprising that he himself reacts angrily to its application. Yet he is so clearly the dominant personality in his generation, and so clearly the outstanding singer that *some* word is required to characterise him. Certainly 'superstar' has too many irrelevant and misleading overtones to be acceptable, and his antipathy to the label must be respected. He is, in any case, the last artist to whom the word should be applied in any personal sense, and the last person to whom it should be applied in an artistic sense – particularly judging by the standards of so many 'genuine' superstars. However one describes him, he remains inescapably a very fine singer and musician, and one whose influence is all-pervasive in the world of British, European and trans-atlantic folksong.

Of similar age and approach, Nic Jones is another guitarist with a basically percussive style, though his later records have shown an increase in a legato technique. With a plainer, but no less thoughtful, singing style Jones has been at pains to avoid the more hackneyed areas of the folk repertoire and has, therefore, always been a refreshing and stimulating singer to hear. He seems to remain unreasonably modest about his fiddle-playing, which he has largely restricted to recording sessions; though his recent group involvement with Bandoggs has resulted in more live work.

(Before I go any further, I should make it clear that almost all the singers whom I shall discuss intensely dislike critical comparisons, feeling that they add little to an appreciation of their music and, in the case of an unfavourable comparison, one way or the other, can actually do harm. While I respect this, any form of evaluation can scarcely avoid comparisons, even if only to give landmarks to the reader; but I shall endeavour to keep such comments as objective as possible, and would emphasise that they are only personal views.)

Dick Gaughan is without doubt the leading young Scottish singer (immediately, a comparison!). With a more flexible guitar style than many of his contemporaries, he has a nakedly raw voice capable of immense passion and, at the same time, great tenderness. His strong accent, which becomes even more marked in singing, does not always make it easy for a non-Scottish audience, and when it is overlaid, as it frequently is, by elaborate vocal ornamentation, it must be admitted that one is often affected by the force of the music rather than by the story-line. The point is, however, that one *is* affected by the music; if it is not too strong a phrase, and to paraphrase Oscar Wilde, Gaughan's singing transcends even the barrier of a common language.

Like Carthy, he is at his finest as a solo performer, and probably as an unaccompanied solo performer, but he has also worked with two widely differing groups – the distinguished Boys of the Lough and the exhilarating Five Hand Reel, a contrast that says much for the range of his approach and ability.

Dave Burland offers a considerable contrast to the three already mentioned. Soft of voice and with a more fluid guitar, he presents a more lyrical side of the folk repertoire, coupled with a small, but stringently chosen, handful of contemporary songs by writers such as Dory Previn and David Ackles. As with Gaughan, when he gives himself the space of an unaccompanied song, his style becomes noticeably more elaborated and ornamented.

Tony Rose is, like Burland, a largely lyrical singer, finding his repertoire largely from the south-west of England, and backing himself on guitar and concertina. The first revivalist singer to avail himself of studio techniques such as double-tracking (now a folk commonplace), he has developed into a fine if unassuming singer; modesty is a refreshingly frequent characteristic of folksingers, and is perhaps one factor at least in the non-commercialisation of the genre.

Of the major singers of the second generation, Peter Bellamy must be one of the most intriguing. With a vocal style initially extremely mannered and now mellowed to the merely markedly individual, he has been a flamboyant and significant figure on the scene in a variety of roles. Originally as the driving force and lead voice in the highly influential group The Young Tradition, later as a solo performer, and more recently still as an exceptional songwriter, he has ploughed a furrow that has become steadily more important, culminating in the composition of the ballad-opera *The Transports* (1977).

The Young Tradition took the glee-singing of the Copper family and brought to its presentation a flair that was more of the pop than of the folk world. Even if slightly exaggerated, there is at least an element of truth in the statement that, if till then, the Revival had been worthy, with The Young Tradition it suddenly became exciting and dramatic. Their impact was considerable, and imitatory groups are in existence today, eight years after the group's demise.

Like The Young Tradition, though without the immediate trendy success, The Watersons have also exercised considerable influence in the sphere of unaccompanied part-singing. In spite of two changes of personnel over the years (the latter bringing Martin Carthy in) they have continued solidly on their way and have maintained and even enhanced their reputation and position. Their one record of their own songs, *Bright Phoebus*, demonstrated that they were strikingly unusual songwriters, but so far they have declined to explore this avenue further. As a soloist, Mike Waterson must be reckoned one of the best male interpreters in the country.

To have singled out those few singers is in itself an act of either considerable courage or extreme foolhardiness, according to your viewpoint, since the folk world possesses plenty more capable of challenging, as it were, for a place in the first division, and plenty of vociferous supporters to form a mini-Kop into the bargain. Indeed, it could be said that there are *better* singers than those I've mentioned, if not so influential. On that score, Jean Redpath must take pride of place with a voice capable of almost infinite gradations from the tragically husky to the stridently dramatic, a voice of superb control and great beauty. Four younger singers – Frankie Armstrong, Alison McMorland, June Tabor and Geordanna McCulloch – are demonstrating already that they are also capable of becoming equally fine singers.

Among the men, there are many excellent musicians who continually attract capacity audiences throughout the country, thorough-going professionals who are the mainstay of the Revival. Short lists would inevitably vary from selector to selector – as they do with Test teams – but none could, I think, omit Robin and Barry Dransfield, Bob Davenport, Vin Garbutt, Roy Harris, Martyn Wyndham-Read, Jon Raven, Chris Foster, Sean Cannon or Archie Fisher. Garbutt, in particular, with his uniquely surrealistic humour and unflagging energy, is typical of the singer-cum-humorist category that has emerged so successfully from the folk clubs. Mike Harding, Billy Connolly, Jasper Carrott and Jake Thackray are other examples.

On the group scene there was at one time considerable strength which is steadily being eroded by a mixture of economic problems and audience apathy. The long-standing electric group Fairport Convention (now called merely Fairport) still survives after a series of personnel changes that make the Plantagenet genealogy look like a straight line. That it still holds on to a major portion of its original drive is to no small degree due to the effect of Dave Swarbrick's driving personality and blazing musical talent.

Steeleye Span collapsed in ruins in 1978; groups such as Horslips, Hedgehog Pie, Lindisfarne and the JSD Band have either died ingloriously or transmuted into something else; now a newer group, Five Hand Reel, dominates the field, though it has not yet broken

through into the commercial world that swallowe\
Steeleye.

Acoustically, it is significant that the major groups are all long-established. The two leading Irish groups, The Chieftains and Na Fili, still play to packed houses, though the former appear to have become a touch jaded – the result, possibly, of a less than happy brush with high-pressure showbiz. In Scotland, groups come and go with remarkable frequency, each being hailed with delight, but none achieving either the success or any signs of the longevity of The Clutha or The Boys of the Lough.

The latter is, in fact, far from being a pure Scottish group, based in Edinburgh though it may be, since the personnel consists of one Englishman, one Shetlander and two Irishmen. Nonetheless, their repertoire incorporates a large percentage of Scottish material (there being a considerable traffic of music between Scotland and Ulster), and it is as a Scottish group that they tend to be regarded. Both their presentation and their performances are apt to be severe – intellectual almost – and they make few gestures towards the popular market. Honesty being quickly recognised in the folk world, they are among the most highly respected of all British musical acts.

The Clutha, in direct musical contrast, are characterised by a superb, raw drive that has remained undiminished and uncompromised throughout their fifteen years of existence. Other bands such as Ossian, The Battlefield Band, New Celeste, Alba, The Whistlebinkies – all these have risen and faded while The Clutha, still only semi-professional, flourish mightily.

The Corries continue on their sophisticated way, as they have done for many years and, like their English counterparts The Spinners, take folk music in palatable form to a mass audience. The McCalmans, too, handle this market with verve and deftness, without so far having alienated the folk world.

In England, many excellent groups have gone to the wall in recent years. Of the survivors, The Yetties are still recognisably folk-orientated though gradually succumbing to the twin pressures of television and eccentric record production. Hedgehog Pie, once an electric group of erratic standards, is now an acoustic trio including Dave Burland; and Bandoggs features three of the best individual acts in the country: Nic Jones, Tony Rose, and Pete and Chris Coe. Only coming together for specific tours or recordings, Bandoggs may well be the shape of the future in this respect – for it is as relatively difficult for an acoustic group to stay on the road as it is for an electric group. Costs may be less, but so are receipts. But whether it is a portent or not, Bandoggs must be regarded as the most important acoustic English group working at the moment; a group that is, for once, at least as great as the sum of its component parts.*

The Tyneside quartet The High Level Ranters remain one of the longest-running groups in England, doubtless sustained by the exceptional quality of the area's traditional music-making.

The British Folk Revival has also become the spark from which other countries have taken light. Similar revivals are currently under way in Norway, Sweden, Denmark, Holland, Belgium, France and Germany; and even in Japan, while there is no revival as such, great interest in folk music of all kinds is being generated.

* Since the time of writing Bandoggs have announced their break-up.

All the European revivals started by using British material, usually sung in English and sometimes even with the appropriate regional accent. British artists tour in those countries regularly, and some are even resident there. But recent years have shown a remarkable increase of interest in the indigenous music, and professional musicians are beginning to research their own traditions. Already France has produced the Breton musician Alan Stivell, the groups Malicorne, Chemin Blanc and La Bamboche, and the outstanding young guitarist and singer Pierre Bensusan. Belgium has produced Rum, a group that toured Britain on several occasions, and 't Kliekske, together with such solo artists as Wannes van der Welde, Hubert Boone and Roland; while Holland has produced Scheepesbeschuit. The German revival, handicapped by the Nazi's use of folk melodies as propaganda, is slowly developing, led by the groups Singspiel, Elster Silberflug and Fidel Michel, with singers and writers such as Hannes Wader, Knut Kiessewetter, Gunther Stossl and the late Peter Rohland.

In America, too, the British influence is felt. Having provided this country with the initial stimulus, the American revival scene now looks to it for both artists and material. Far more English artists tour there than Americans tour Britain, and British records are eagerly snapped up as they appear: an acknowledgment, perhaps, of the fact that many of their folksongs came originally from Britain.

If I had been writing these pages only a few years ago, I could at this point have summed up the achievements of the song revival in glowing terms and pointed to a glorious future. The achievements *have* been considerable indeed. The Revival has given to many songs not just the safety and the permanence of print and recording, but, more importantly, has also restored them to active use. It has created an audience which is involved, aware and intelligent; it has provided an alternative entertainment which should be self-perpetuating. It has contributed significantly to teaching methods in various disciplines, with critic-editors such as Roy Palmer and Jon Raven constructing educational books of great stimulation and flair.

But there does seem to have been a decline recently, a slowing-down. Part of the trouble, people say, is that so few promising young singers are emerging, but this is only partly true. What is more worrying to my mind is the general air of apathy that seems to have wrapped itself round artist and audience alike. This is not to say The End is Nigh; there is more than sufficient life in the Revival yet for it to pick itself up and dust itself off just as efficiently as Fred Astaire. Everything has its ups and downs and provided the basic *willingness* persists – and particularly the willingness of those unsung and largely unpaid heroes, the club organisers – I see no reason why the movement should not happily celebrate its half-centenary in due course.

Apathy is an insidious thing. It is difficult to isolate, and difficult to cure. But the solution is not to be found in dropping out, or in gimmickry, or in awhoring after strange gods. If the solution lies anywhere, it is in continued quality.

The Instrumental Revival

The opening years of the Revival were not remarkable for the standard of instrumental playing; accompaniments were workmanlike rather than brilliant, and soloists were few and far between. But with the advent of the second generation, the instrumental revival got under way.

Inevitably, the emphasis was on the guitar, which had quickly established its overwhelming dominance as first choice of instrument, and virtually the only permanent effect left by the influences of skiffle and the American singers. A new breed of guitarist sprang up, one midway between the three-chord specialists and the pop-orientated guitarists such as Bert Weedon and Diz Disley. Experimentation in tunings became a commonplace, and techniques improved rapidly, to the point where several of the major figures of the next few years were instrumentalists who sang rather than singers who accompanied themselves. And inevitably, for a period, there was a wave of technically brilliant musicians who often had little to do with folk music *per se*, but who performed in that context simply because the folk world was the world of the acoustic guitar. Musicians such as Isaac Guillory, Gordon Giltrap, John James, Bert Jansch, John Renbourn and Davey Graham permanently expanded the frontiers of folk guitar playing, even though much of what they played was contemporary and even original. Their stylistic influence was and still is considerable.

Notwithstanding the often tenuous relationship, folk guitar also improved out of all recognition. Martin Carthy was the first in the field to explore the possibilities of open tuning, to be copied by countless others; and among his generation Nic Jones, Dave Burland,

Dick Gaughan and, latterly, Martin Simpson have raised the art of accompaniment to a high level. One can make the criticism that too much emphasis is laid on the percussive aspect of the guitar's tonalities and too little on the liquid *legato*, but there are signs that this emphasis is diminishing; the added range of timbres can only add further effectiveness to an already well-harvested area. On the fringes of the English folk scene, the American Dave Qualey and the Frenchman Pierre Bensusan are demonstrating a more flexible grasp of the guitar's complete potentialities.

If the guitar is an imported instrument, the fiddle is at least native – with some others – to the British and Irish traditions. To a lesser degree (a ratio related closely to the difficulty of playing it well) it has also established itself as one of the main instruments of the Revival, usually in a group context. In England Dave Swarbrick and Peter Knight have been the dominant figures here, though Nic Jones and Barry Dransfield have made considerable contributions, the former mainly in the field of recordings.

In Scotland and Ireland, where the instrumental tradition has been much more continuous, the fiddle's position is more integrated, and is related more closely to the dance than to concert bands. Erlend Voy and Calum Allan of The Clutha, for instance, are prime examples of young musicians who are so steeped in traditional music that it is difficult to define whether they are traditional or revivalist musicians. And the young Shetlander Aly Bain lies so close to his native tradition that he spends as much time with local Shetland musicians as with his professional group The Boys of the Lough. Taught by the doyen of Shetland fiddlers, Tom Anderson, Bain is and will remain a key figure in the instrumental history of the Revival.

In Ireland, Matt Cranitch of Na Fili and Martin

Fay of The Chieftains also present problems of definition for the same reasons. In countries where there has been little need of a revival, the dividing line is inevitably thin. Indeed, one is possibly stretching a considerable point to include either of these two groups in a consideration of revival music. If there is a point of contrast, it must be in the professionalism that both display – professionalism not merely in the sense of earning a living by playing, but also, and more importantly – in the area of presentation. There is a rehearsed quality about them that is absent in the wholly traditional bands, but which can be seen at its clearest in the case of The Boys of the Lough, where the underlying thoughtfulness is even a key factor in their music.

The re-establishment of the 'squeeze-box' family, after its decline in the earlier years of the century, has also been notable. Much of it, however, has been due not so much to auto-regeneration of interest as to a commercially-inspired campaign. Nonetheless, the melodeon, the English and Anglo-German concertinas and the accordion have all in varying degrees reasserted themselves as revivalist instruments. But if the main flowering of interest has been the result of pressure, one person clearly ante-dates this situation. Alistair Anderson's technique on the English concertina must be described as virtuoso, however much one dislikes using such a strong superlative. In his work with The High Level Ranters and as a soloist, Anderson has both explored and extended the repertoire of the instrument as no other person has done. Many people are competent on the concertina, but Anderson comes in a league by himself, as far as the world of folk music is concerned. John Kirkpatrick comes close to challenging him in terms of technique, and certainly surpasses him in terms of variety of instruments, but Anderson's single-minded devotion to one instrument has allowed a greater investigation in depth of his instrument's capabilities and idiom.

Apart from Anderson and Kirkpatrick, the concertina family is used mainly as self-accompanying instruments by the more traditionally-minded of the revivalist singers. Louis Killen, Tony Rose and Peter Bellamy are three of its main exponents in this respect.

Various other 'unfashionable' instruments have been revived by young musicians. In a trend largely led by Peggy Seeger, the Appalachian dulcimer has appeared in Britain, being played by stylists as far apart as the traditionally-orientated Sandra Kerr and the contemporary songwriter Allan Taylor (the latter using it slung like a guitar and playing it as such). This instrument too has its virtuoso, who has created a new language and repertoire for it. Roger Nicholson is, I think, the first significantly to use the dulcimer as a solo instrument so all-embracingly as to call on the services of such composers as Bach.

The hammered dulcimer has also been rediscovered, though the brunt of its revival has been on the shoulders of the veteran Jimmy Cooper, whose death in 1978 was as unexpected as it was lamentable. Among the younger revivalist musicians, Chris Coe and David Kettlewell now carry its further revival forward.

The once-humble penny or tin whistle – now made in stainless steel for the experts – has had less of an impact than might be expected, considering its portability and relative simplicity to the level of competence. Vin Garbutt, John Doonan and Bob Pegg have all presented it to a high degree of efficiency, but for the most part its use seems to be confined to being a tuning device for unaccompanied groups. This is not true in Ireland, where its use remains natural among revivalist as among traditional musicians.

Many other instruments have been flirted with,

ranging from the hurdy-hurdy to the jew's harp. Most have merely displayed to a new generation why they fell into disuse earlier, though John Wright has undeniably brought a new dimension to the jew's harp. Andy Cronshaw has concocted and developed an amplified zither, but its uses in the context of British folk music have so far been limited. Mandolas, bouzoukis, mandolins, pandoras, lute-guitars and various other imported instruments have also appeared, but their use remains essentially limited in numbers. In most cases, they are played like guitars and the net effect is therefore of slightly strange-sounding and strange-looking guitars. (I have, in fact, also seen a ukelele played like a guitar; the effect was horrific!)

I have not so far mentioned the pipes, either Scottish, Northumbrian or Irish. It is said that it takes twenty-one years to make a piper, and the Folk Revival is barely that old. There *are* young pipers, it is true, notably Colin Ross of The High Level Ranters and Jimmy Anderson of The Clutha. But in the main the revivalist pipers – and there are few – tend to be of an older generation than their guitar-strumming or fiddling colleagues. Any form of pipes is a testing instrument and it is significant that the two leading Irish pipers – Paddy Moloney of The Chieftains and Tomas O Canainn of Na Fili – are both noticeably older than the average folk musician. It is significant also that the majority of Scottish pipers stand outside the Revival, being brought up in a tradition of their own. Musicians such as John Burgess and John McLellan carry on the piping tradition in their own way, and the popularity or otherwise of the pipes in Scotland owes nothing whatsoever to the Folk Revival. (One can understand this, of course: a set of great pipes going at full blast in the confines of the average folk club would be something for only the fanatics.)

There is always the danger in any revival movement that the kiss of life will be carried out for its own sake, whether the corpse is actually capable of revivification or not. Some medieval instruments have been dragged protesting from their well-merited obscurity for another tour of duty, only to reveal their original limitations all over again. The crumhorn, the cornetto, the rebec, the vielle and others have all been pressed into service in a largely self-defeating attempt to rediscover folk roots. By and large, however, the instrumental side of the Folk Revival has displayed a gratifying degree of commonsense and has led to a standard of playing that bodes well for future generations.

Work in the Regions

Folk music, by its very nature, is very much a local and regional phenomenon. A Somerset version of a folksong can differ considerably from a Shropshire version of the same song; and, by extension, Scottish and English variants can be even more radically different. Both songs and dance music have always been studied on a regional basis, and it is only right that the research work currently in progress within the Revival should be considered on the same basis.

It should be clear that, even though field research must be carried out locally, the existence of an available central archive is essential for the collation of individual projects and, where necessary, to initiate work on a controlled basis. Scotland, Ireland and Wales are fortunate in possessing such centres, and it is wholly typical of England that it has none. The Vaughan Williams Library of the English Folk Dance and Song Society has the nucleus of a national archive, but lack of funds and space hamstring any major development. In any case, it is a private library and a national archive should be state-owned or, at the least, owned or financed by a major university.

It gives me no pleasure as an Englishman to observe that the English have always been notoriously apathetic towards their native arts. Composers have been forced, as often as not, to adopt foreign styles to make any impact during their lifetimes; Elgar and Vaughan Williams are the only two major figures who have at all developed an English style. Painters have been largely ignored (except, in more recent times, as cheap investments) until their deaths; poets have not even had the benefit of canvases to sell. Although we have both a

National Theatre and a heavily-sponsored central opera house, the latter especially pays far more attention to foreign than domestic works.

It is therefore only to be expected that the country has not seen fit to have a School of English Studies, nor any organised scheme of research and investigation. Such work as is done is done on an individual basis, with occasional small Arts Council grants and subsidies made available. Nor is there a national academic journal where findings may be published for further discussion. Researchers are forced to work largely in a vacuum, with only personal relationships and contacts to supply points of comparison and co-operation. Under such lamentable conditions, it is surprising, perhaps, that so much good work is being done in England, and it says much for the doggedness of the people concerned.

For the sake of convenience, I would like to divide the country into five fairly arbitrary regions: the north-east, the north-west, the Midlands, the south and East Anglia. I am only to aware that this presents its own anomalies (such as lumping Yorkshire in with Tyne-Tees and Cleveland) but it is also the least cumbersome way to present a broad picture of what is happening.

In the south, the figure of Peter Kennedy dominates the scene, though it is barely accurate to describe him as a southern collector, working as he does all over the British Isles; the fact that his home is in Devon is almost irrelevant in the face of such a broad sweep of activity.

Kennedy was born into a family actively engaged in the study of folk music. Marjorie Kennedy-Fraser was his great-aunt, his mother was the first Secretary of the English Folk Dance Society, and her sister, Maud Karpeles, was Sharp's chief collaborator and a mainstay of the EFDSS for many years. He initiated the BBC series *As I Roved Out* and contributed many of the songs broadcast during its long run. His massive *Folksongs of Britain and Ireland* (Cassell, 1975) is undeniably the most representative and best-annotated selection of songs so far published, and virtually the only one to touch upon such sub-cultures as Manx Gaelic and Channel Islands French.

Kennedy is now the Principal of the Centre for Oral Traditions at Dartington, where he is steadily making available in both printed and cassette form the results of his many years' collecting. As an active collector, Kennedy seems now to have retired, for the amount of collation, analysis and preparation involved in organising his enormous amount of field research is clearly a task of considerable magnitude.

Working more specifically in the south of England, and in particular in the Home Counties, Mike Yates has been producing impeccably documented recordings of music of the travellers. One of the most experienced of all the younger collectors, Yates seems to be possessed of an enviable talent for discovering unknown singers and persuading them not only to sing, but also to talk freely – not always an easy task when one is a non-gypsy among gypsies. *Inter alia*, his work has demonstrated – as has similar work in Scotland – how much the living tradition of this country is in the hands of the travellers, who seem now to have a larger store of variants of English songs than of gypsy songs.

Moving up-country to East Anglia, we have a truly contemporary situation where all the significant research is being done for release on LP. The 'singing pubs' of The Ship and The Eel's Foot at Blaxhall have both undergone the presence of microphones for the capture of the still-existing musical evenings in the bar, and two records have been released. Like most uncontrolled live recordings – there are ways and ways of producing live recordings – extraneous noise limits the entertainment aspect of the recordings, but they remain valuable archive material.

Slightly further north, in Norfolk, the repertoire and memories of Walter Pardon are still being thoroughly researched. Two magnificent records have been released by Leader Records, and a certain amount of documentary material has been published by Peter Bellamy. In earlier years a song book would have appeared; now not only the songs, but also the voice, the mannerisms, the very style of Walter Pardon are available for enjoyment and study.

The Midlands presents a slightly anomalous picture, boasting as it does an extremely lively Revival scene but, since the death in 1975 of Cecilia Costello, no traditional singers of major significance, unless Shropshire is included in the area to bring in Fred Jordan. Jordan, like Pardon, has been recorded and studied at length, and over a longer period. His original repertoire seems to have been more limited than that of Walter Pardon, and, as I have observed earlier, he has recently taken to learning new songs from recordings of other artists.

The most important work in the Midlands is being done at one remove, as it were, from the tradition itself. Both Roy Palmer and Jon Raven are in the course of an exhaustive continuing study of both the songs and the folklore of the area. Both have contributed to the excellent Batsford *Folklore of the British Isles* series, as well as producing both song collections and other critical and analytical works. Both have also worked extensively in the educational field, using a stimulating technique of juxtaposing songs with contemporary reports of historical events. In this field, Palmer's *A Touch on the Times* (Penguin, 1974) is a superb patchwork of social change between the years 1770 and 1914, using little-known photographs as backing material. By the same token, his study of the soldier's life between 1750 and 1900 (*The Rambling Soldier*, Penguin, 1977) using often unpublished accounts of military life and the wars of the period, possesses a rare quality of evocation.

Jon Raven, based in Wolverhampton (Palmer lives in Birmingham) has also produced an array of song-books and through-written texts, culminating in his self-published but completely professional *Urban and Industrial Songs of the Black Country and Birmingham* (Broadside, 1978). Unlike Palmer, however, he also backs up his books with recordings released on his own label, also called Broadside; among the topics he has explored in these joint fields are canals and the navvies, sport, railways, the nail-making industry and the Industrial Revolution.

In the north-west Paul Adams and his Fellside Recordings have at least begun an examination of the local songs, a process begun some years earlier by Tradition Records, a little further south. So far most of Adams' work has been in libraries, but some of the results have been released on record by revivalist sing-ers. Apart from some beagling and fox-hunting packs who have kept alive their hunt songs, little is known at the moment about the likely repertoire of the area *in toto*.

The north-east, in comparison, has always been a hotbed of activity, both in traditional and revivalist terms, and to a far larger extent than elsewhere in England the two streams have frequently merged. Young instrumentalists like Colin Ross, Alistair Anderson and Johnny Handle have recovered many tunes from both old players such as Billy Pigg and from early printed collections. As all three belong to The High Level Ranters, their newly-acquired tunes tend to be used practically rather than presented as research results, a practice that is, in itself, an indication of the closeness to its roots of the Revival of this area.

In the adjoining county of Yorkshire, Bill Leader (eponymous hero of Leader Records) has, since he settled in the county a few years ago, been steadily examining various aspects of folk culture in a series of unusual and revealing records. His album of the songs of the Holme Valley beagle pack, for instance, and that of various largely unknown Christmas carols recorded in local pubs, have indicated yet again that there is still a fertile substratum of activity even in this day and age where field research can make striking yields. Further, his recording in 1977 of the hitherto unknown Yorkshire traditional singer Frank Hinchcliffe has suggested that the wide-open Yorkshire spaces could well be investigated in greater depth.

Turning to Wales, we have a situation where little is known of folksong outside Wales while there is still a very active tradition within. The language barrier creates difficulties, of course, but it is an unfortunate fact that even twenty-five years of the Folk Revival have not added to England's limited knowledge of 'The Ash Grove' and 'David of the White Rock' (except for 'Hymns and Anthems', possibly!) Nevertheless, the Welsh Folk Museum has been recording traditional music for some years now, and the first recordings were released in 1978. They are excellently documented, complete with the essential translations, and provide the outside world with the first hints of musical riches far beyond the male voice choir and Cardiff Arms Park. The recording programme is in the hands of the small Welsh label Sain.

I have already observed that the traditional situation in both Ireland and Scotland is much stronger than that in England, comforting though the latter undoubtedly still is. Both countries have national organisations to sponsor research and study, though in both cases funds are by no means unlimited.

In Scotland, the School of Scottish Studies spearheads and largely masterminds folk studies in Scotland, Orkney and Shetland. It is perhaps ironic that much of its earlier work was done by the Dane Thorkild Knudsen, while one of its senior staff-members is an Englishman called Peter Cooke, himself a specialist in African studies. Cooke has, in fact, adapted himself remarkably well to his new field and set up the extremely fine series of recordings now being released by Tangent Records.

The high priest of Scottish folk studies, though, is Hamish Henderson, a poet of considerable achievement and writer of many songs that have already passed into the tradition, especially the 'John McLean March' and 'The 51st Division's Farewell to Sicily'. His collation of the many verses of 'The D-Day Dodgers' is another such. Henderson's discoveries in the field of Scottish folk music are almost legion, beginning as they do with the towering figure of Jeannie Robertson and proceeding by way of Jimmy MacBeath, the Stewarts and Willie Scott, to name only a few. His written work on the subject, however, has been lamentably small so far.

Much basic work of considerable worth was done in the earlier days of the Revival by one of Henderson's disciples, Arthur Argo, who is credited with the collecting of many now-standard Scots folksongs. Again, while he has recorded, written work is hard to find.

Finally, one must mention the lengthy study in depth of the Stewart family, currently being brought to a conclusion by Ewan MacColl and Peggy Seeger. The repertoire of these families and others has already been published (*Travellers' songs from England and Scotland*, Routledge and Kegan Paul, 1977), and the companion study of the Stewarts themselves is due shortly. Like Henderson, MacColl has done tremendous work in

Scotland, but until the appearance of these two books there has been little in print though much on record. The emphasis is characteristic of 1970s research.

In Ireland the Comhaltas Ceoltoiri Eireann is the organising body for folk research; like the School of Scottish Studies, its tape archive is now considerable, and much of the groundwork has been done by Tom Munelly, a young collector of quite prodigious energy and an encyclopaedic knowledge of Irish culture. And if the organisation itself is not in the forefront in terms of recorded releases (as is its Scottish counterpart), at least the repertoire and the artists are being presented to the world by smaller independent companies such as the English Topic label, and a group of Irish labels including Mulligan, Claddagh and Dara. Indeed, it seems sometimes as if everyone who even toys with a concertina, fiddle or whistle in Ireland has been recorded, so frequently do the records appear. Certainly, at the time of writing, Irish music – particularly instrumental music – is fashionable in British Revival circles, an interest indicated by the frequent Topic releases, and the Irish collecting work of the young English collector Roly Brown.

In terms of formal national interest, then, it is clear that the Celtic countries are actively involved in the preservation and dissemination of their folk cultures. Only in England do we fail to make the effort, relying on the work of small record labels and individual researchers. But folk music is undeniably a minority interest, and it is difficult for commercial companies working solely in the field of folk music to make ends meet. If Topic and Leader do so manage, it is only through intense economies and a great deal of dedication – which, in practical terms, means that the people concerned are a long way from making fortunes. This, of course, accords neatly with the English concept that being involved in any form of the arts means self-sacrifice; and further, without self-sacrifice you are no good anyway. This is an attitude that we as a nation have had for centuries now, and probably much of the blame must rest on the narrow shoulders of Thomas Chatterton and his post-mortem romanticisation; but however it arose or whatever was originally used as a justification, *it is purely and simply a handy way of avoiding responsibilities*. If artists work best while starving in garrets, then let us help them by making them do so. Conversely, any creative artist who makes money is not a great artist; he can't be because if he were he would be starving. In particular reference, any folk-singer who makes money is clearly corrupt – and that is an attitude the folk world knows only too well.

It is an appalling standpoint, and the worst thing about it is that any government of whatever persuasion can only too easily find ready-made excuses for finding other priorities. For instance, international copyright agreements made in the mid-sixties have *still* not been ratified by our governments since then, and there is no sign of any impending revision either. There will always be something more important.

Maybe there are many in the folk world who will prefer things to remain this way, with government keeping clear of involvement. I happen to believe that it is a shame to England that it cannot find the pride in a great tradition to provide a central facility for its study and preservation.

And that is a remarkably fine example, I suppose, of a voice crying in the wilderness.

Practical Aspects of the Revival

Traditional song centred on the village pub, and it is no coincidence that the Folk Revival does likewise; the interdependence of beer and song has always been strong and will doubtless continue so. Indeed, the close relationship that has sprung up in recent years between the folk festivals and CAMRA is as natural as Marks' love for Spencer.

In choosing the back rooms of pubs as venues for folk clubs, organisers are by no means aping the past. The resident singers do not sit in inglenooks – and would not even if inglenooks were to be found – and neither do they sing where they sit. The overriding reason for selecting pubs is an immediate source of beer – and those pubs which serve real ale stand the best chance of acquiring a club.

In the first two or three years of the Revival, during the mid- to late fifties, there was no more than a handful of clubs across the country. At the time of writing, a reasonable estimate would give a figure of around seventeen hundred. Most meet weekly at or towards the end of the week (for obvious reasons) though a few are fortnightly. Audiences can be as small as forty or fifty, and as large as two or three hundred. And there are almost as many *kinds* of clubs as Polonius had categories of play. At one end of the spectrum the traditional clubs do not mean quite what they say – they book revivalist singers, but the repertoire is virtually entirely traditional. Some contemporary songs in a traditional style may creep in – if the club books an artist like Peter Bellamy or Cyril Tawney, both singer

86

and songwriter – but the emphasis is heavily on the real thing. Some clubs – few and growing fewer – will concentrate on contemporary songs and white blues; but as with all general groupings the weight of the samples falls in the middle, into a booking policy that can and usually does embrace everyone from the genuine traditional musician through the middle-of-the-road artists to the blues-based singers and comics. The folk scene is nothing if not eclectic, just as traditional music itself was. And even the most respected of revivalist singers can break into a Presley or Beatles song as an encore – not to mention those of John Denver, James Taylor or The Eagles.

The structure of a club evening tends to be unvarying wherever you go – and this is one of the weaknesses of the system as a whole. The evening is opened by the resident artist or artists, who warm the audience up; they are followed by others, indistinguishable from the residents except in the context of club organisation, called floorsingers. Their allotment is usually two songs, and it is with these short spots that the floorsinger gains sufficient experience to graduate to residency or even to full-fledged professional status. The first half closes with half an hour from the booked guest, if there is one. After a beer break, the second half follows the pattern of the first.

The drawback of this kind of presentation is its rigidity, coupled with the fact that too few floorsingers and residents learn new songs with sufficient speed. One hears too frequently the statements 'I sang this last week but . . .' and 'I only learned this one today so I may forget it'. Ewan MacColl once said that a singer should learn a new song every week; a counsel of perfection, indeed, and I would not expect an amateur singer to live up to that testing demand. But a song a month is surely within anyone's capability, and a repertoire of twenty songs ensures at least a diminution of the unblushing repetition that is one of the worst hazards of regular attendance at a club. Some clubs are fortunate in possessing a resident group of near-professional standards – the Nottingham Traditional Music Club, for instance, or the Grimsby club, are two such – but these are few and far between. The vast majority of clubs have to make do with singers of lesser quality and, as such things are self-feeding, a lesser quality seems to produce musical stasis just as much as a higher produces a continuous improvement.

Such a relatively minor matter would not normally call for extended comment were it not for the unfortunate fact that it has considerable effect on long-term membership and attendance. If a club is in decline, the reason can normally be found in its residents. If they are content to churn out the same old songs week after week, they can hardly be surprised when they start churning them out to smaller and smaller audiences. It is a basic and obvious truth, but it is one against which many resident singers are complacently blinkered.

Admission to the club ranges between 40p–70p, on average, but this often fluctuates according to the artist booked and how much his fee is. In recent years, the charges made by both artists and clubs have fallen desperately behind the steadily increasing cost of living. Clubs complain when artists raise their fees, and artists complain because clubs drag their feet in increasing *theirs*.

A club with an audience of fifty, each paying 50p (though floorsingers are frequently allowed in free) grosses £25. If the room has to be paid for, and if there are publicity charges, then these must be met before the artist can be paid. Even if there are no other calls on the club's income, £25 is still an appallingly low payment for a good professional singer. To be able to

88

pay £35, the club must have a minimum audience of seventy, and so on in proportion. But some acts are duos, trios or quartets, and neither two, three nor four can live as cheaply as one.

On the artist's side, his fee is very much of a gross. A successful folk-singer may work twenty to twenty-five nights a month. To do this he has to travel the length and breadth of the country; indeed, he must travel virtually all day and sing in the evening, usually not finishing until eleven pm or later. If he works five nights in one week for a fee of £30 – a reasonable average – his gross for the week is £150, making an annual income of £7,700 if he worked at that pressure every week of the year. Quite impressive. Or at least it is until you start deducting all his expenses: instruments and car insurance (and the latter can be punitive for a professional musician), food, accommodation, National Insurance, income tax, telephone, postage, agent's commission if he has one.

If we consider actual figures relating to one of the leading British singers, Alex Campbell, the weight of these expenses can be clearly seen. The figures relate to 1975, but are still representative.

	£
Fares	1,817.71
Accommodation	375.00
Food	884.00
Commission	797.15
Publicity	219.50
Accountants' fees	113.99
Postage	161.99
Instruments	96.92
Telephone	351.57
National Insurance	128.82
TOTAL	4,946.65

Those expenses were accumulated in the course of travelling 42,205 miles in nine countries. In that year, Campbell made two records, appeared at two festivals, did six radio broadcasts in three countries and a television documentary. He made 215 live appearances, 2 at festivals, 29 concerts and 184 club bookings. He spent 257 days and nights away from home, spent 1,438 hours 55 minutes travelling, 305 hours 50 minutes on stage and an estimated 620 non-singing hours in clubs.

One or two comments on the expenses are extremely revealing. The charges for accommodation and food would be very much higher if it were not for the fact that many kind people put him up for the night. The commission would be higher if his wife did not do a lot of work on his bookings. The sum of £96.22 on instruments is *purely* for strings, picks and mouth harps: during that year he bought no instruments and needed no major repair work.

And if you compare his work hours (including travelling time) with the British average of 233 days and 1,920 hours per year, it will be obvious that Campbell – like his colleagues – works extremely hard for only a moderate net earning.

As I have said, many clubs have been reluctant to raise their charges to an economic level, fearing that attendances will drop off. But one can barely get into a cinema nowadays for under £1, and two pints of beer and a packet of cigarettes will cost about the same; while concerts, theatre and the like cost a great deal more. So it is really a question of adjusting to unpalatable facts. If professional singers are going to survive to give their entertainment, sufficient money must be raised to pay them a living wage. That is the situation *tout court*, and no amount of havering or ostriching will make it go away. It is a problem that is fairly and squarely in the laps of the club organisers, and they must solve it if they want to continue to survive in their present form.

The professional folk-singer lives a pretty gruelling life, and the more successful he is the more hectic it becomes. For a singer, 'stardom' doesn't mean the possibility of long runs in one place, or a lucrative film; it just means more bookings, more one-night stands in distant parts of the country. I sometimes wonder why they do it, but I am grateful they do.

The standard folk festival starts on a Friday evening and runs through to Sunday evening. The smaller ones may last only a day and involve only two or three artists, while the longest, at Sidmouth, lasts a week and involves dozens. The biggest, Cambridge, has attracted up to 17,000 over the weekend, approaching a pop festival in size if not in atmosphere. There is, fortunately, a considerable difference between pop and folk festivals. At the latter, even the largest, there is a relaxed and friendly air about the proceedings, as if the occasion were really an outing for the staff of a huge company. The artists mingle freely with the audience, a tendency calculated to give palpitations to the average pop bodyguard. There is no hassle, the police are thin on the ground, and there is a notable absence of drugs. Folkies drug themselves on, if anything, real ale and Newcastle Brown, and the temporary fashion for pot has long left the scene.

Now, if one thing has come out of all the foregoing, it is the essential smallness of scale that exists in the folk world. Individual audiences tend to be small, admission charges and artists' fees are small, the scene itself is small – festivals are more like reunions than anything else, in many cases. And it is this very intimacy that has probably preserved the Folk Revival from the depredations of the mass media and Tin Pan

Alley – a place, incidentally, that no longer exists as a music centre though it remains as a handy catch-all.

To the popular music publisher, folk music is essentially 'long-hair', and as such something to be considered only when it is adapted, for instance as the signature of a popular television series or a film. Performing royalties from folk clubs and festivals are small beer indeed in the context of the overall performing right royalties collected in Britain – last year in the region of £17,000,000. So for purely financial considerations the music publishers have stayed away, except for the occasional production of singalong books aimed at a market I have never yet been able to identify.

Only at the pop end of the folk spectrum, involving artists like Ralph McTell and Steeleye Span, is there any high pressure involvement on the part of publishers, managers and the media. Anything below that is dismissed as unimportant – and very thankful the entire folk world is, too! Visions of what happened both to the trad jazz revival and skiffle remain only too clear in the memory: natural popularity, followed by the media and the promoters, quickly and inevitably followed by exhaustion and collapse. The audiences are sated by over-exposure, the musicians worn out by pressure of work; only the manipulators come off best, and there is always something else for them to move on to.

And in the absence of big money, the disinterest of the mass media is a natural concomitant. Only *Melody Maker* among the national popular music weeklies carries regular folk coverage, and this is restricted to about two pages an issue. *Sounds* and *New Musical Express* have both stopped their columns, and the others have never been interested at all. There are no glossy monthlies on the subject: only *Folk Review* and the much more recent tabloid *Folk News*. The BBC presented the minimum possible – one programme a week – for a long time, but there are signs now that it is taking folk music much more seriously as an established minority interest, though there is still a long way to go before it receives a coverage comparable to jazz. Both radio and television are offering more programmes, though – probably inevitably and unchangeably – the artists presented are taken from the more sophisticated end of the spectrum. There has yet to be a television programme that presents the Revival as it is, though Radio Two's long-running *Folkweave* has faithfully reflected both the excellences and the faults of the clubs for over seven years.

BBC local radio also supports the folk movement in the various station areas. Most stations run weekly or fortnightly programmes; not all, however, have a high local content, but prefer to be mini-*Folkweaves*.

In the face of this general disinterest from the moulders of taste, one is almost tempted to ask how the Folk Revival has survived so long. The simple answer is that the disinterest is *precisely* why. But there are a number of reasons. Firstly, there is a highly effective grapevine which deals not just with gossip, but also – and more importantly – with emerging musicians. A successful early booking in the south can lead directly to bookings elsewhere in the country, and a good appearance at a small festival can provide several subsequent club bookings.

Secondly, there is the inherent sturdy independence of the average folk fan. He or she tends to be of above average education and intelligence, is reasonably knowledgeable about the music, and is not easily conned. All the hype in the world will not force a musician on a folk fan if several hearings have shown that he is no good. Stage gimmickry tends to get the folk fan's back up; for him or her the music is the important thing.

And thirdly, if it is not too fanciful, folk music has always been a sort of 'underground' music. As we have already seen, the working classes were held separate by their 'superiors' in earlier generations, and little was known of their music by the gentry, let alone the nobility. Traditional music does not need high-powered patronage to survive; indeed, high-powered patronage can all too easily be a point of distortion. The Victorian collectors fortunately failed in their attempt to 'civilise' folk music and introduce it into the drawing-room and the classroom; and equally fortunately there has been no serious attempt to 'popularise' it in recent years. However frustrated the fans may feel about the slender dissemination channels, they can count themselves lucky that big business has not taken folksong and wrung it dry. In historical terms, it might have been a majority interest at one time, but it is not now, and will never be so again.

And this, at the risk of sounding élitist, is surely all to the good.

New Developments

In the upper and middle classes' relationship with folk music, there has always been an element of *de haut en bas*, so that when folk music has been taken into the big house, as it were, it has been with a distinct air of 'improvement', rather as if a village waif had been adopted and given the run of the kitchen. This was very much a concomitant of the times, of course, and nothing else could have been expected; but the attitude did lead to unnecessary falsification and distortion. Even innocent bawdiness was suppressed and rewritten by Sharp, Baring-Gould and others, while on the musical front the various piano arrangements by Lucy Broadwood and others endeavoured to turn folksong into *lieder*. Even some fifty years later Benjamin Britten used them as accompaniments to over-intellectualised piano pieces.

The Folk Revival itself has also seen attempts to dress folk up for presentation to a wider and different audience; some have been genuine endeavours, some have been mere gimmicks. The two main avenues of experimentation have been a retrogression into a medievalism not always perfectly understood by its practitioners, and a movement towards certain elements of rock music. More recently still, the young French musician Pierre Bensusan has been using a free jazz approach with some success, but this is an isolated case.

Both of the main trends can be said to have been initiated largely by the same artist – unexpectedly, one of the most traditionally-orientated of the younger singers, Shirley Collins.

In 1969, in a record entitled *Anthems in Eden*, she

presented fourteen songs (plus two instrumentals) accompanied by a group of largely non-folk musicians employing viols, rebecs, crumhorns, sackbuts, portative organ and recorders. This album, together with its sequel *Love, Death and the Lady* (1970) had an enormous impact on other singers and musicians. Several medieval-type consorts sprang up, featuring obsolete instruments and playing a mixture of early music and folksong. Trevor Crozier's Broken Consort, Amazing Blondel (who, I thought, displayed such a staggering ignorance about their music and their instruments that their failure seemed to be automatic, swift and ignominious) and, latterly Gryphon and City Waites have all tried. Only the last two made any real headway – City Waites by playing the music without unnecessary frills, and Gryphon by creating the Polonian category of medieval-folk-rock.

If this sub-branch of the Revival has now largely withered, the reason is not hard to find. The instruments used are largely obsolete, and only used now in specialist antiquarian performances. And if they were jettisoned by earlier generations, it was because they lacked the flexibility called for by the increasing sophistication of music in the eighteenth and nineteenth centuries. Once the novelty of the sound is over, therefore, there remain few areas for a continuance of development, and the music quickly becomes sterile because it lacks the essential core of rightness; it is neither creatively progressive nor constructively re-creative.

A few musicians continue to use medieval instruments, but these are now used merely as adjuncts and not as a *raison d'être*. The avenue has been explored and found to be largely a dead end. However, one valid endeavour arose indirectly from this approach, the superb two-record ballad opera *The Transports*

96

(1977) by Peter Bellamy. With a consort of musicians directed by Shirley Collins' sister Dolly, this major folk work used its material – both original and traditional – with respect, love and intelligence. While it scarcely represents a justification for further exploration of the field, the fact that it has triumphantly transferred to stage performance indicates that it has an inner strength which relies not at all on studio techniques.

Shirley Collins was also involved in one other significant exploration of the boundaries of folk when she produced in 1964, with the guitarist Davey Graham, an album entitled *Folk Roots, New Routes*. Not everybody appreciated this record for what it was, or the pointers it gave, for it was probably a decade ahead of its time in its subtle blending of traditional English song with such foreign elements as Indian music, blues and jazz. If this record is respected now, it is largely as a matter of hindsight, and even now its message has not been investigated fully.

At about the same time as the appearance of the two medieval Shirley Collins records, the first undercurrents of electrification began to be felt in the folk world. Those two records supplied an impetus here also, in that they explored for the first time the possibilities of new sonorities, accompaniments that were neither classical nor pseudo-classical in approach, and that broke away from the already omnipotent acoustic guitar.

Fairport Convention – still one of the most inventive of the early electric bands – was formed in 1967, but only achieved their full potential when they were joined in 1969 by fiddler and mandolinist Dave Swarbrick who, for some years previously, had been playing with the Ian Campbell Folk Group. With his technical brilliance and extensive knowledge of the British folk repertoire added, Fairport's third record *Liege and Lief* became an immediate rallying-point for the more progressive of the folk musicians. It is difficult now, when there have been so many electric groups of varying qualities, to recapture the exhilaration then generated by that band. Even now, after many changes of personnel, but still with Swarbrick at the helm, they remain among the small handful of bands that can generate genuine excitement.

If Fairport can claim the longest continuous life of any electric group, the band that captured most public attention during the eight years of its life was Steeleye Span. Formed in 1970, they resisted for a long time the beckoning of the rock world, remaining closer to the feeling of the tradition than Fairport, who were always heavier and, in some ways, more brash. Indeed, Steeleye did not even have a drummer until 1974, though they had added various percussion parts on some records before then. At the height of their musical quality (though not of their popularity) the group consisted of Peter Knight (fiddle and occasional percussion), Martin Carthy (lead guitar, vocals), Tim Hart (guitar, dulcimer, occasional vocals), Ashley Hutchings (bass guitar) and Maddy Prior (vocals). A major change of direction took place when Carthy and Hutchings left, and were replaced by Bob Johnson and Rick Kemp, two rock musicians, and, a little later, by rock drummer Nigel Pegrim. From then on the music tended to become heavier, and they expanded their act away from the purely musical, incorporating dances, mumming plays and even back-projected films in the act, together with encores that were a strange mixture of rock and barbershop quartet – a gesture towards the mass audience that many people found ill-advised. They also began to take liberties with traditional texts, a lack of respect that they would never have shown in their earlier days. At this point, an ever-diminishing circle became obvious and, though they finally attracted a huge audience, the pressures became too much and the group fizzled out in 1978.

If these two groups have dominated electric folk since the start of the trend, there have been plenty of lesser and shorter-lived lights. The Glasgow-based JSD Band offered a raw and gutsy excitement for a while before drifting into the rocks; and the Irish groups Horslips and Spud presented their national folk rock with some temporary success.

The electric quartet Mr Fox (Bob and Carole Pegg, Barry Lyons and Alan Eden) had a short, but tempestuous, life which probably did no good to Bob Pegg's songwriting talent, but nevertheless created a minor watershed: an arch-traditionalist embracing contemporary techniques not only fluttered the dovecotes, but also showed that an amalgam *was* possible.

Pentangle too moved into this uneasy field, managing to survive for a respectable time before succumbing to sheer inanition. The group (Bert Jansch, John Renbourn, Jacqui McShee, Danny Thompson and Terry Cox) demonstrated that diverse talents cannot always synthesise, but on a number of occasions (notably on *Jack Orion*) produced some excellent and worthwhile music.

The Albion Country Band/The Albion Dance Band/The Albion Band perhaps offered most in its variegated existence. Formed as The Albion Country Band by Ashley Hutchings after his departure from Steeleye Span (just as Steeleye was at least partly a spin-off following his departure from Fairport), the first Albion realised during its sadly short life far more of the true potential of electric folk music than any other band that has come together. Their firm adherence to a traditional repertoire (though occasional bows were made in the direction of contemporary folk while Richard Thompson and Steve Ashley were with the band); the consummate artistry they displayed at their height, when outstanding musicians such as Martin Carthy, John Kirkpatrick and Simon Nicol were members; and, possibly, most of all, the vitalising association with the Albion Morris Team, a splinter group from the Chingford Morris; these were the qualities which led to a style of playing that was wholly English in approach, traditional in outlook and joyful in spirit. Sadly, they rarely managed to play at their peak; when they did, they provided a powerful vindication for the electric performance of folk music.

The Albion Country Band died, and Hutchings spent a short time organising the Etchingham Steam Band, a wholly acoustic group, before forming the Albion Dance Band. This was a group of variable strength, according to who was available; at its full strength it had nine players, including two percussionists, and it included a leavening of classical medieval musicians. No band of that size could ever play on a regular basis, and its appearances were restricted to large ceilidhs and concerts, as well as records. In spite of the band's size, Hutchings managed to retain the freshness and the vitality of the Country Band; and, indeed, with this band he probably reached the high-water mark of his career to date. At the time of writing, the band has been renamed The Albion Band, seems to have succumbed finally to transatlantic influences, and is playing mediocre mainstream rock.

Among the few electric bands now in existence – the economics of keeping an electric band on the road are daunting – one must consider the Scottish–Irish Five Hand Reel as the most outstanding, though the recent departure of Dick Gaughan must inevitably have a major effect. Though capable of using full power as heavily as any other electric group, Five Hand Reel are also thoughtful enough to resist the temptation of using mere volume to whip up excitement, and are even willing to play and revivify gentle drawing-room folksongs such as 'My love is like a red, red rose' – a gesture akin to a young English artist singing 'Dashing away with the smoothing-iron' or 'Bobby Shafto'. Though much more recent then the other groups discussed, Five Hand Reel have, I think, already proved their point.

The question remains: does the electrification of folksong have any valid justification, and is it more than a merely temporary gimmick?

If groups such as Albion (in its early days), Steeleye, Fairport and Five Hand Reel can occasionally add a new dimension to old songs – and can present them with some success even to a non-folk audience – I think this must be taken as at least a partial justification for the experiment. For a while they managed to approach what must have been the early spirit of performance, and managed to generate an excitement that had not been felt since the early days of the Revival. Naturally enough, they have not escaped the accusation that they have corrupted and cheapened traditional music, that in some way they are in the process of killing it. But folk music has survived many vicissitudes – not least the Industrial Revolution – and it possesses an inner strength and a capacity for self-renewal (indeed, instant and constant self-renewal.) As Vaughan Williams wrote in *English Folk Songs* (1912): 'A folk song is like a tree, whose stem dates back from immemorial times, but which continually puts out new shoots. . . . In one aspect folk song is as old as time itself; in another aspect it is no older than the singer who sang it.' To my mind, arrangers like Lucy Broadwood and Benjamin Britten cheapened folk music far more than the electric bands are likely to, for they managed to devitalise it, to turn it into something it is not, a twee middle-class entertainment. Folk music is essentially a music of guts and life, and these qualities the electric groups have certainly preserved; even, on occasions, added to.

Nonetheless, I suspect that it too will eventually prove to be a dead end. Already there are indications of an intellectualisation which is alien to the atmosphere of folk music; and if this comes about, sterility will follow as it did in the attempted medievalisation of folk. Popular electric groups must also fight against the mental and physical staleness that is the inevitable concomitant of extended tours and one-night stands, the inescapable by-products of commercial success – and, since electric groups are using the language of pop music, it follows that, whether they deny it or not, they are implicitly seeking commercial success to some degree; and *need* to, to survive.

Like the so-called 'trad' jazz of the sixties, electric folk may well wear out its batteries. When it does, it is comforting to know that the original songs are, like Mole's old home, still there, fresh, alive and unsullied.

Contemporary Song

Like most artistic movements, the British Folk Revival has had its share of controversies: accompanied or unaccompanied, political or non-political, electric or acoustic. None, however, has had quite the divisive effect of the vexed question of 'contemporary folksong'. While the other arguments raise their heads occasionally, this one is a continuous cry raised by the hardcore traditionalists who resent the encroachment into folk clubs of songs that they regard as 'pop'.

In spite of this – and even in spite of a degree of justification in their attitude – it would be foolish for several reasons to attempt to consider the Revival in terms of traditional music only. Whether the traditionalists like it or not, contemporary song has secured more than a toehold in the Revival's history and it is, in fact, sometimes difficult to see how the Revival could have survived economically without it.

In the first place, the traditionalist exclusivity derives from an error in historical perspective – an error into which the nineteenth- and early twentieth-century collectors also fell: that of imposing an essentially middle-class judgment as to what should constitute a singer's repertoire. Judging by the published collections of the period, the village singers offered a diet of purely traditional songs. In fact, of course, they were omnivorous, singing anything that took their fancy from the worlds of music hall, popular song or, in an earlier period, the stately home and the royal court. To be sure, there is strong evidence to suggest that many singers distinguished between traditional song and the rest (and this was largely a quality judgment), but their function in the community was to entertain, and if the song was good enough it was sung. Many music hall and vaudeville songs must now be considered as absorbed into the tradition; and, indeed, to argue otherwise is to imply that the tradition stopped short at some arbitrary date. (When?)

Further, protagonists of contemporary song would maintain that the folk clubs have, in effect if not in intention, taken over from the working men's clubs which, where they still exist, have become more sophisticated establishments, sometimes booking the latest transatlantic superstar and owning their own breweries. While the thesis cannot be wholly supported, there is a good deal of truth in it. In spite of attempts to prove the contrary, the Revival has always been an essentially middle-class movement, and if there was initially a left-wing intellectual impetus (which I shall discuss more fully later) that impetus has now largely died out. From that point of view, the parallel is not a close one. It is in the more general area of function that similarities appear: the self-organised, participatory, community activity of a folk club is extremely close to the original working men's clubs in both atmosphere and achievement. Both can be classed as sub-cultural activities, closely related to the community, but not of official status; and both protect and foster a popular art-form.

Like it or not, it does folk culture in its widest sense no good to impose what is, in effect, a subtle form of artistic censorship. One cannot say 'This is not good, this is not what you should be listening to.' One cannot guide tradition; tradition evolves by itself. To attempt to protect, however benevolently, courts paralysis. Few things suffocate more effectively than cotton wool.

But there are other, more recent, reasons for accepting that contemporary song has a role to play in the Revival.

During the 1950s, the skiffle craze used much contemporary material, and that influence has remained. Another reason can be found in the personalities and involvements of some of the major figures of those early days.

Foremost among these is Ewan MacColl, whose personal history is almost archetypal. Born into a Scottish working-class family, he learned his music in the traditional way from his parents. '[My father] was always interested in singing from the time he was a young man, and he had a huge repertoire of songs, *not just traditional songs* (my italics – FW). I suppose you could say his repertoire consisted of a big body of Scottish traditional songs (that is, the classic repertoire of traditional songs), ballads, lyrical songs . . . a lot of Burns material. But he also had a hell of a lot of urban Scots material too . . .

'[My mother] knew a lot of songs, but hardly any of the urban songs he knew. She had a big stock of ballads, and a hell of a lot of children's lore – singing games, for instance . . .

'I suppose I assimilated a lot of these songs rather than learned them consciously – assimilated them almost by a process of osmosis. And I was also interested very early on in writing songs.'

As a young man, MacColl was also involved in left-wing street theatre, and by the early 1930s had already written songs like 'The Manchester Rambler', which he wrote for a mass trespass over Kinderscout and which is still one of his most frequently performed songs.

Much of the Revival's early emphasis on British material was due to MacColl's insistence that singers should strive for a national identity; and much of the relevance of contemporary song in the Revival is due to his own achievements in this field. By the early 1950s,

MacColl, with Peggy Seeger, A. L. Lloyd, Seamus Ennis and others, dominated and virtually directed the Revival. And a considerable, though by no means always overt, part of the direction was political. The protest song did not, contrary to some apparent beliefs, start with Dylan or even with Woody Guthrie; and neither MacColl's personal history nor his political persuasions could allow him to ignore this area of the tradition. So, among the traditional songs and ballads, appeared the contemporary protest song.

In spite of Arthur O'Shaughnessy's beliefs to the contrary, however, songs do not have any noticeable effect on the life of a country, and this aspect of contemporary song in the context of the Revival has now largely died down. There are still a number of songwriters such as Leon Rosselson and Alex Glasgow, who concentrate on the political or social, but such songs are not often heard in the clubs – unless, of course, the guest artist is himself a songwriter in this genre. Similarly, one or two song magazines still publish protest songs, though these usually fail to catch on – due, probably, to a consistently boring stridency. This does not apply, however, to some of the socially-motivated songs of MacColl, which still enjoy great popularity, simply because they are fine songs *qua* songs, regardless of any message they might carry.

Nevertheless, whatever the status of political songs nowadays, their original contribution to the Revival was considerable, and they remain one of the factors behind the continued general acceptance of non-traditional repertoire in the clubs. Even now, a degree of social awareness, even if not always politically inspired, is one distinguishing mark of the contemporary folksong.

There is another reason, and it is one that many of the arch-traditionalists resent more than anything else.

This is, quite simply, the fact that the folk world now-adays offers virtually the only possibility of musical apprenticeship in the various fields generally bracketed casually under the title of 'popular'. Until the advent of instant entertainment, as evidenced in television and the 45-rpm single, would-be entertainers learned their craft in the many halls and clubs round the country. For one reason or another, these have now died out, and success tends to be achieved – transiently, more often than not – through the contributions of the record producer and promotions expert. While this system of sudden stardom can throw up occasional artists who are genuinely talented, the majority can have little practical experience in their chosen profession; and there are not a few casualties – some fatal – littering the last few years of the pop scene to testify to the trauma of such a situation.

There are, however, artists who do not immediately seem to fit this ritual, either because they do not want to, or because they genuinely want to *learn* the job of entertainment in its widest sense. For such as these, the folk clubs offer just about the only way of gaining the necessary experience. The complaint is, therefore, that fledgling pop stars and songwriters batten on to the Revival and the clubs as a means of furthering their own careers elsewhere. If many expressions of this complaint become quite unnecessarily hysterical (with wild talk about the corruption of folk music), the point itself contains a certain amount of truth. The clubs *are* the only practicable training ground for young songwriters, and particularly for writers of quality songs. For them the doors of the pop world tend to remain closed and, in any case, the whole approach of the folk audience is closer to that of the quality songwriter than the largely mindless world of pop.

Once in a while, singer–songwriters will emerge

from the folk world into the wider one of popular song. Ralph McTell, for instance, learned his craft in the folk clubs and has only recently achieved major success in commercial circles. It is ironic, perhaps, that his success should come largely through an old song, 'The Streets of London', long regarded in the folk world as a 'standard' while remaining largely unknown outside that sphere.

The hardcore traditionalist will merely say that the absence of other training grounds is not his problem, and that the contemporary songwriters should stay away from the folk clubs. But, as we have already seen, Bronson seems implicitly to accept that contemporary song has a potential place in the folksong tradition.

Moreover, such an attitude on the part of the traditionalist can be said to be merely faint-hearted, as it seems to imply an expectation of corruption; nothing is less likely. The folk audience is, in any case, both involved and aware, and does not take kindly to inferior products. Such contemporary songs as manage to survive on the club circuit tend to be the work of craftsmen of a surprisingly high standard, for all their relative youth. And by no means every young songwriter who attempts to enter the folk world is accepted. Evidently, in practical terms, some songs are eligible as potential contemporary folksongs while others are not. It is not *entirely* a quality judgment either, as many fine popular songwriters never achieve any sort of acceptance: established figures such as Neil Sedaka, Tony Hatch and Neil Diamond are simply not represented in the club repertoire, while the songs of Gordon Lightfoot, Randy Newman and James Taylor are quite frequently performed. (Interestingly, while Bob Dylan is still accepted as a major influence, especially in historical terms, one does not often actually hear his songs in the clubs now, except for a threadbare handful of titles. To an extent this may be due to an appreciable falling-off in his standards during the past few years, but it is also partly, I think, that his songs are simply not hard-wearing.)

On the surface, there does not appear to be any immediately apparent quality present in the one category that is absent in the other. Yet a distinction clearly exists in the collective mind of the folk audience, and it is sufficiently strong to permit generalisations such as I have just made. It is also sufficiently strong to eliminate the likelihood of mere caprice.

The overall repertoire to be heard in folk clubs ranges from unaccompanied ballads to songs that are in many respects indistinguishable from out-and-out pop music. Yet, as I have indicated, certain implicit guidelines seem to exist, even if they have not yet been satisfactorily defined. It should, however, be possible to isolate them and attempt to reach some preliminary indication (at least) of the qualities of contemporary folksong.

It should be clearly understood at this point that I am not saying that whatever qualities I ascribe to contemporary folksong are necessarily absent from other categories, notably pop music. Of course they can be present in both, and often are. What I *am* saying is that the folk audience seems to *demand* these qualities, in a way that the pop audience does not. The one is a music to be listened to positively; the other is a music to be heard.

The qualities required, it seems to me, are: melodic and lyrical competence (to put it no higher); a recognisable melodic structure; intelligence; literacy; integrity.

Now I am well aware that this list can be described both as basic and pompous, according to one's view. To be sure, they *are* basic – given any sort of musical awareness on the part of an audience. And to be equally sure, it is probably pompous to list them in that way. Nevertheless, it is the presence and interaction of these admittedly basic qualities that distinguishes the contemporary folksong from the normal pop song. For acceptance as that implies that the song has *enduring* qualities, far removed in both effect and intention from the mayfly pop song. And if that comment seems to admit the songs of such writers as Cole Porter, Irving Berlin and Noel Coward, so be it – at least in terms of potentiality. It would not be the first time in the history of folk music that *good* popular songs found themselves absorbed into the tradition.

If the requirements are basic, they are also stringent, for they demand something that is more than a mere time-waster. They therefore constitute a basic split between the world of pop and contemporary folksong – as far as audiences are concerned. Even though there is a limited – indeed, *highly* limited – cross-circulation of songs between the two worlds, it is difficult to imagine the repertoire of (say) The Clash flourishing in the folk clubs, just as it is difficult to imagine the survival in the pop world of songs by writers such as Bill Caddick or Dave Goulder.

The question doubtless remains: what makes a contemporary folksong? Certain common qualities clearly exist, and the matter does seem to rest partly on considerations of style and partly on quality. As I have observed earlier, certain popular and even 'pop' songs (there is a considerable difference) are capable of achieving acceptance – *as they always have been* – though the practical differentiations that arise can sometimes be baffling to the casual observer.

By the same token, accepted artists can be rejected if they turn their backs too blatantly on folksong standards and attitudes. The judgements are again elastic and even quirky; sometimes they seem to depend at least in part on the personality of the artist concerned. Ralph McTell, for instance, has not taken conventional club bookings for some years now, yet he is still cherished by folk audiences; others, less unassuming, more bustling, can be turned away very promptly indeed.

The folk audience is an aware one, which likes order and clarity (clearly a traditional legacy); it demands in its songs a structural competence, literacy, intelligence; it will not be played down to. Songs that it approves are likely to find themselves taken into the tradition of the future. And the validity of this is something, as Bronson commented, 'to which Child . . . might have become reconciled'.

I have already cited Ralph McTell, and probably the qualities I have been discussing can be most clearly seen in his work. Still only in his early thirties, McTell learned his craft busking in the streets of Paris and on the British folk club circuit. Although he now has a wider success, his songs have been a minor cult for some years among the *cognoscenti*, and especially in the folk clubs. His justly famous 'Streets of London' is one such; unfortunately, perhaps, he wrote it early in his career and now views it much as the older Yeats viewed 'The Lake Isle of Innisfree'.

If there is one dominant theme in McTell's work, it is a casting-back to innocence in its various forms: memories of and the re-creation of childhood are constant factors. So also is a more generalised nostalgia for times past through which an innocence is apparent if not explicit. In the extreme case of 'Michael in the Garden' the innocence even appears as autism.

The nostalgia for childhood – and for sharing present childhood (particularly that of his son) is the most common single theme, though. And of this category, the most specific is 'Barges', in which McTell re-creates a sunlit childhood day with his brother:

'Me and my brother returned to the water,
    I saw a pike that was two feet long;
    Two small magicians each with a jam-jar
    Cast spells on the water with hazel-twig wands.'

McTell's latest work has perhaps shown a diminution of the nostalgic element, and where it shows it is sometimes a secondhand and dubious nostalgia only. In the musically attractive 'Maginot Waltz', for instance, he is sufficiently careless as to date the Maginot Line in World War I, and for me at least the song is weakened by the error.

If McTell looks back to childhood and its joys, the songs of Cyril Tawney look back largely to his days as a submariner. He is far from being a prolific composer; apart from occasional four-line comic squibs, his last song dates from 1970. Nevertheless, he is still very much one of the major songwriters to emerge during the period of the Revival. His classic songs – 'Sammy's Bar', 'Sally Free and Easy', 'Chicken on a Raft', 'Grey Funnel Line' – either date from or reflect his time as a sailor; and of his twenty-six songs currently in print, exactly half are concerned with the Royal Navy.

Unlike McTell, Tawney tends to work within traditional frameworks, both lyrically and melodically. In 'Sammy's Bar' the placing of the refrains at the second and fourth lines is a common structural device in traditional song; and the construction and atmosphere of the lugubrious 'On a Monday Morning' resemble traditional song in their economy and bluntness:

'My lover she lies asleep
My lover is warm and her heart is mellow
I'd trade you the world just to share her pillow
On a Monday morning.'

'Sally Free and Easy', a song dating from 1958 and Tawney's most-performed song – and frequently misinterpreted through lack of appreciation of precisely this point – is also based strongly on a tradition, that of the negro blues. Tawney himself has described the song as a 'full-blooded holler', which emphasises this element in the song – present not only in structure, but in feeling.

Tawney's melodies seem to have an archetypal quality: although the lyrical structure is often closely related to traditional forms, the music – carefully and elegantly shaped – does not always seem to have the same obvious connections. Indeed, some of his songs seem to descend from the better quality ballads of the twenties and thirties. There is about them a timeless quality, completely free from the shifts of musical fashion and yet speaking with an entirely individual voice.

If Cyril Tawney's naval songs can be taken as occupational songs (in the folk sense), so also can the earlier songs of Dave Goulder. Brought up in the industrial environment of Nottingham, Goulder's first links were with the railways, on which he worked as a fireman. The songs relating to this period of his life established him as a songwriter of considerable potential, particularly in the eyes of other musicians. In public terms, little was known of him as he rarely left the Ross-shire glen where, until a few years ago, he ran a mountaineering hostel; nevertheless his song 'January Man' was immediately accepted as one of the outstanding songs written during the Revival period. It is, indeed, a remarkable song, written specifically for unaccompanied singing and lyrically so accomplished that it is now taught in schools as a poem.

The transition from the industrial Midlands to the Torridon mountains inevitably provided Goulder with another source of raw material. In this later phase he produced many fine songs on natural themes, though few were idyllic. Indeed, and perhaps aptly for a man who lived in such rugged terrain, some even tended towards the macabre; Goulder is not an experienced naturalist for nothing. In his accurately sinister dialogue 'The Raven and the Crow' the natural behaviour of the birds is used to build up a cumulative picture of brooding threat:

'The hawk will murder as she flies, the falcon hurtles from the skies,
But the hoody waits to take the eyes when the eyes can barely see.'

Goulder's control and use of the macabre is one of his strongest assets; the characteristic is totally individual in the field of contemporary folksong though the influence of the tradition has prompted many attempts in the genre. One of his more recent songs, 'The Sexton and the Carpenter' is *comédie noire* at its best (or worst).

At the same time, it would be misleading to over-emphasise this aspect of Goulder's work. Songs such as 'When They Laid You in the Earth' (a title reminiscent of Henry Purcell, though the song's content is very different), 'Cold Unfriendly Way' and 'Sandwood Down to Kyle' display a longing and a warmth that occasionally seem to be lacking in much contemporary song.

The songs of Harvey Andrews present a more complex picture. It is reasonably accurate to say that he first made a national reputation with his early protest songs: in particular 'Sandy', his lament for the death of Sandy Scheuer, accidentally killed in the Kent State University shootings of 1970. His next major song, however, inadvertently created a controversy which, for a while, clearly damaged Andrews' standing and viability. 'Soldier', in spite of an unambiguous sleeve-note, was widely interpreted as a pro-establishment glorification of military heroism and, therefore, by left-wing logical extension, of authoritarian violence; whereas in fact it was a simple (if lyrically somewhat overwritten) story of a young man caught in an impossible situation. The song was neither for the British authorities nor against the Irish rebels; it was about the senselessness of violence, applied on a personal level.

Most of Andrews' early songs were written entirely by him, but in 1973 he began the first of a series of collaborations, working with other songwriters such as Graham Cooper, Geoff Bodenham, Pete Wingfield and John Dunkerley, whose tragically early death destroyed a more than promising partnership. Andrews returned to solo writing, but with his range and instrumental technique noticeably improved.

As a corpus, the songs offer a wildly fluctuating view. They range from the melodramatically abrasive 'Headlines' to romantic pop-style songs like 'Jane' and 'A Little Moon 'n' Juning'; and although much of his own beliefs are expressed in his political and social songs these have tended to be less successful *as songs*, with the exception of 'Unaccompanied'. Making the point is clearly important to Andrews, but to my mind he is more successful when he allows his lyrical side to show more clearly. His most recent songs, including the lengthy but powerful 'Lot 407', show signs of a welcome synthesis.

If Harvey Andrews' Belfast song ('Soldier') was not a

lasting success (though it remains popular, for obvious reasons, with army audiences in Ulster and Germany), Allan Taylor's 'Belfast '71' – now renamed 'Lead On, I'll Follow' – has remained extremely popular. One reason is implicit in the revised title – the song itself is not so particularised or personalised as is 'Soldier' – and another lies in the fact that it is a chorus song. The same applies to Taylor's other war song, 'The Morning Lies Heavy on Me', written on his brother-in-law's departure for Vietnam.

But Taylor is predominantly a lyrical composer. In his earlier songs there was a strong medieval element, more recently transmuted into a compound of Tudor polyphony, English traditional song, and the English music of such composers as Vaughan Williams and George Butterworth. His brief flirtation with a group, the ill-balanced Cajun Moon, seems to have left few scars, and Taylor's most recent record (*The Traveller*, 1978) confirms his position as one of the most attractive and worthwhile songwriters in the field.

If the songwriters considered above offer a representative cross-section of the current work going on in the field of contemporary folksong, this is not to suggest that no others exist worthy of mention. At the more commercial, pop-biased end of the spectrum, the songs of Richard Thompson are probably foremost. 'Meet on the Ledge' and 'The New St George' (the latter a rare example of traditional influence in his work) are frequently performed and have received several cover-recordings; and other, more recent, titles are already gaining a wide currency. Thompson himself is a brooding, enigmatic figure on the folk scene, standing somewhat outside it stylistically yet closely involved musically and instrumentally – to the extent that he has been a member of both Fairport Convention and the Albion Country Band.

Unlike those so far mentioned, the songs of Rosemary Hardman spring almost entirely from her emotions. Happily, she is saved from categorisation as 'yet another girl singer-songwriter' (a category that unfortunately exists and owes nothing to male chauvinism) by her extrovert performances and the degree to which her lyrics manage to become externalised. Although many of them are *chansons à clef*, possession of the key adds very little to one's understanding and appreciation. The protagonists of 'Firebird' or 'Marazion Sands' are important as catalysts only; their identity, once the song has been written, is irrelevant.

In spite of the fact that her songs are among the most personal of all contemporary folksongs, Rosemary Hardman appears to have the greatest potential for truly popular success outside the confines of the folk world, being (in some ways at least) part of the line that runs from Marie Lloyd. If the other songwriters are all, to an extent, intellectual writers – certainly as compared to the purely 'gut' writer – her songs have a directness and a simplicity that permit instant and instinctive communication.

The turbulent, striving figure of Bob Pegg must also be mentioned. Moving from the field of revivalist singing into the electric contemporary field, with a group called Mr Fox, Pegg has consistently explored what are generally considered to be the outer limits of folk. 'The Gypsy', a straightforward narrative song that frequently ran over fifteen minutes in performance, was one of the most famous experiments of the sixties, foreshadowing his important through-composed *The Shipbuilder* (1972–4). This forty-five minute 'oratorio' (I place the word in quotes because the work is unclassifiable in terms of conventional musical categories) is a skilful blending of original though traditionally-orientated story, interpolated traditional songs used as dramatic and psychological devices, electric and multi-tracked instrumentation, and heavily Gothic overtones. It remains unique in the field in spite of other superficially similar experiments such as Fairport's *John Babbacombe Lee* (1971) and the Peter Knight–Bob Johnson fantasy *The King of Elfland's Daughter* (1977).

If theatricality is one aspect of Pegg's work, it is also, in a more direct sense, at the core of Jeremy Taylor's songs. Taylor came to folksong from the theatre, where he appeared in revue and wrote the music for several shows, including *Mrs Wilson's Diary*; his recent two-man shows with Spike Milligan have tended to return him to the stage although he has maintained a close connection with the folk clubs. Many of his songs are satirical, clearly deriving from the 'point number' of intimate revue; their subjects range from transplants through cruelty to children to the horror of 'The Red Velvet Steering-Wheel-Cover Driver', a manifestation only too familiar to anyone who drives.

The songs of Alex Atterson present a stylistic problem in that they derive more closely from art songs, and are therefore musically at a fair remove from folk. Nonetheless, Atterson works in the folk club context and his work must be considered as part of the club music. The majority of his songs are settings of the poems of Charles Causley, himself very much a folk poet in that his poems are frequently written in ballad form, and possess inherent folk qualities. In writing these songs, Atterson has subordinated himself to such a degree that some of his songs are beyond his own singing capacity. Recorded versions have begun to show their potential, however, and, with no disrespect to Atterson, future recordings will hopefully be by trained singers. At the moment all one can say is that the songs, especially the Causley settings, transcend the normal stylistic barriers and, if a sport on the folk scene, nevertheless suggest that Atterson could be a songwriter of more general significance.

While there is a great deal going on at that end of the spectrum there is, if anything, even more when we come to consider those composers working in an overtly traditional or quasi-traditional style. Many of the songs in this genre are, in fact, mere adaptations of actual traditional songs, and almost as many tend inevitably towards pastiche; but in a gratifying number of cases the writers are achieving an individual voice within the framework.

In terms of scope and adventurousness, the work of Peter Bellamy must, I think, be considered first. Originally a revivalist singer, Bellamy first turned to songwriting in 1970, when his love of the works of Rudyard Kipling – and in particular the Puck books – prompted him into setting the poems from those two books. The resulting record *Oak, Ash and Thorn*, though stimulating, was uneven and consisted largely of adaptations of existing tunes. Two years later, with *Merlin's Isle of Gramarye*, he completed the round-up of the Puck songs in a series of settings that were strikingly more original and complex. Copyright difficulties caused a delay of some five years before his *Barrackroom Ballads* could be recorded; and these finally confirmed his major status as a songwriter in the genre. Even his new settings of words long associated with music, such as 'Mandalay', showed an immediate rightness, and his folk-based style skilfully reinforced the already traditionally-inclined poems.

More, however, was to come; and in 1977 his ballad opera *The Transports* was released on record, performed by some of the folk world's leading singers and enhanced with tasteful period arrangements by Dolly Collins. Within a matter of months, subsequent stage presentations in Britain and on the Continent led to a wider acceptance as a superb compound of original theme, words and music in a traditional, but nonetheless recognisably personal, style. At the time of writing it remains unchallenged as the most significant single piece of creative work since the Revival began.

With the exception of 'Farewell to the Land', Bellamy's songs have tended to look to the past. So too, in another way, have those of Bill Caddick, who has devoted a whole record (*Sunny Memories*) to an evocation of Edwardian England. Other songs such as 'Poor Pig', 'Rough Band' and 'Oller Boller' also look back to past customs and lost ways of life, though with no sense of false sentimentality: there is a realism about his nostalgia that makes it bitter-sweet indeed.

By contrast, Matt McGinn – a Scottish Woody Guthrie – was firmly rooted in the present and, in particular, in the politics and social conditions of the present. Like Guthrie, he overwrote drastically and many of his songs are mere squibs; but he achieved a unique position in the folk world as being recognised by the general public in Scotland as one of 'their' songwriters, to the extent that the mere mention of his name on a live Pete Murray broadcast drew a spontaneous round of applause.

The work of Sydney Carter tends to present a rather enigmatic face to the world. Although his output is considerable, his fame rests largely on a handful of songs: his celebration of the London sewerage system 'Down Below', a haunting love song 'Port Mahon' and the immensely popular 'Lord of the Dance' – though this last is not strictly an original composition in the musical sense, being an adaptation of the old Shaker hymn 'Simple Gifts'. Many of Carter's songs are comparable with these three, in fact, even though they remain less well-known and largely unsung except by their writer; and Carter enjoys a considerable reputation among the young folk-singers.

Roger Watson and Alan Bell represent the best of the generation now in its middle thirties to middle forties. Their songs are stylistically based on folk, and their themes are frequently folk themes or extensions thereof; but neither is aggressively so. Watson's 'Sunday Hare', while a parody of the conventional hare-hunting songs, owes considerably more to the music hall than to genuine folksong, while Alan Bell's best-known song 'Bread and Fishes' avoids stylistic categorisation altogether.

Similarly, the team of John Conolly and Bill Meek (who also write equally successfully when apart) provides an interesting example of how non-professionals can secure a considerable reputation in the folk world. Songs such as 'Fiddler's Green', 'Punch and Judy Man', 'Charlie in the Meadow' and others are sung and recorded both in this country and abroad, in spite of the fact that neither of the writers, nor their group The Broadside, finds it possible to do any extended touring whatsoever. The folk grapevine, however, has scattered their songs wide, and the quality is equally widely recognised. A limited fame, perhaps, but a solid one, and that situation is characteristic of the folk world at large.

The songwriters so far discussed – along with, *inter alia*, Vin Garbutt, Peter Bond, Peter Coe, Martin Graebe, John Pole, Phil Colclough and Miles Wootton – represent the main generations now working. Some are still in their twenties, though most are older; but only Cyril Tawney and Sydney Carter straddle the gap between them and the towering figure of Ewan MacColl.

Taken in their entirety, MacColl's songs are a wildly uneven corpus. Many of them – it could almost be said, *too* many of them – are political and social songs of little or no lasting merit except possibly the dialectic. Many are protest songs indissolubly wedded to a specific event and, as such, are as irrelevant now as an old political cartoon (which, indeed, they resemble). Some of them, however, gained a certain status in their day: 'Go Down, Ye Murderers', for instance, was a factor in the fight to clear Timothy Evans' name specifically and against capital punishment generally. A few have managed to retain their relevance and popularity through superb tunes and sufficiently generalised lyrics: 'The Manchester Rambler' is a case in point.

The majority of the songs on which MacColl's song-writing reputation rests, however, derive from the famous Radio Ballads commissioned by the BBC during the first half of the 1960s. From these eight programmes (and the subsequent six records) came the many magnificent songs still sung by professional and amateur alike: 'Shoals of Herring', 'The Big Hewer', 'Schoolday's End', 'Freeborn Man', 'Thirty-foot Trailer', 'Moving-on Song' – these and others, whether judged by the standards of folksong, popular song or even art song, are undeniably outstanding achievements. Though, like Cyril Tawney, MacColl has produced nothing to compare with them for some time now, he remains a major songwriter and a potent influence on the younger generations of composers. Ironically, he is still largely unknown outside the folk world, apart from his work in the field of drama, in spite of his massive international success in 1973 with several recordings of 'The First Time Ever I Saw Your Face' (written in 1957) and the resultant Ivor Novello Award.

*

The two-pronged position of contemporary song in the realm of folk music today illustrates both the basic dichotomy and the eclectic strength of the movement generally. The fact that the songs are written now, by known people, is largely irrelevant. There was a time when 'Lilliburlero' was contemporary, and there will also be a time (hopefully) when some at least of the songs written today will have been absorbed into the tradition, whether the writers remain known or not. Indeed, many are already in the process of being so absorbed, and continuous improvisatory processes are already making their mark. It is arbitrary, to say the least, to state now that a song is or is not a folksong. Only time and the song itself will eventually decide.

Postscript

Well, that was all very interesting, but if it's as healthy and glowing as you say, how come I keep reading in the popular music Press and elsewhere that the Revival is dying on its feet? There seems to be a need for the publication of a regular jeremiad, and isn't this a case of smoke and fire?

Leaving aside the fact that there's nothing like a good gloom to create controversy and improve circulation, no movement – particularly one that started out in such high evangelical fervour as the Revival – can hope to sustain a steady course at any level. Any artistic process is necessarily cyclic, and if the initial fervour has lessened, it's scarcely to be wondered at. But this doesn't mean that the Revival is dying on its feet – or anywhere else.

But it's true, isn't it, that there aren't the new young singers and musicians coming along – the Carthys, the Joneses, the Swarbricks? And if there isn't a further generation of executants coming along, even more burden is going to be placed on the shoulders of the existing musicians and – with the best will in the world – staleness is <u>bound</u> to creep in.

As I've just said, it's a cyclic matter. You can't *expect* to produce top-class anything *all* the time, be it music or drama or sport or whatever. And the mass media – this is particularly true of the popular musical papers – have conditioned us to expect a 'new wave' or a 'significant development' every few weeks. But the values of pop music are not the values of folk music, nor of the Folk Revival.

But in any case, there *are* new people coming forward – people like Martin Simpson, Tim Laycock, Pat Ryan, Downes and Beer, Graham and Eileen Pratt, to name a few. Not a great many, it's true, but it's futile to expect a *continuing* interest to spark as many talents as a newly exploding one.

But I'll accept that we have become a touch involuted. The British are notoriously insular and, by and large, we don't know a great deal about what's going on beyond our shores. Most of the European countries, the United States and Canada, Australia and New Zealand, not to mention Japan, are closer in spirit to the Revival's early days than *we* are, simply because they have looked outwards beyond themselves to what we have achieved, and taken inspiration from it. Maybe it's time, therefore, to look abroad ourselves and derive some new strength from what's happening elsewhere. How many people in this country know anything about the north-west European musicians, other than the few groups whom we've invited across? Whenever they visit these shores they make a considerable impact – but instead of learning the lesson, we merely say to ourselves gosh-isn't-that-remarkable-they-play-good-folk in a superior sort of way and forget about them till next time.

Granted that we tend to be patronising about it, isn't the other side of that coin our complacency towards our <u>own</u> music? Don't we seem to say 'Well, we've got the Revival and if we pay our entrance fee every week that's our job done', rather as the country did when we put the Labour Party in power after the war and then sat back and let them get on with it – forgetting that a two-way effort was needed?

I agree it's always easier to be passive and maybe the Revival is at a passive stage. And this applies to artists and residents and audiences alike. I've already mentioned some of the faults, but there's no harm in reiteration. There's the failure to keep on learning new songs, for a start – and that applies particularly to residents and floorsingers – and of keeping songs in one's repertoire for too long. There's nothing meritorious in learning a new song for its own sake, whether it's good or bad, but there is a necessary consideration for the audience.

Then there's the rigidity of the club evening. If everyone knows the guest artist won't be on till nine o'clock, they'll tend to come in then – which gives the residents a derisory audience and doesn't exactly offer encouragement to up-and-coming singers.

And then there's the sheer amateurishness of some professional singers, who are professional only in the sense that they get paid. It's all been said before – arriving late; going on stage without being tuned-up; long, rambling, incoherent introductions; the forgetting of words; poor enunciation of both spoken and sung words; untidy and even dirty turn-out. *A professional actor, for instance, simply wouldn't get any jobs if he committed the same faults.* Singers should have the courtesy – and it comes down to just that old-fashioned quality – to rehearse their presentation just as much as they rehearse their songs.

So far you seem to be agreeing with me all down the line. What future has the Revival got, then? What about the electrics, for example?

Economics are against the continued existence of the electric bands unless they can hit the big time – and if they do that it's a different game of skittles altogether, with different conditions prevailing. To keep a band on the road full-time is hideously expensive, especially in the context of the clubs – in fact, it's pretty well impossible – so from the purely practical point of view I can't see any substantial future in that direction. Electric bands will continue to exist and will doubtless do valuable work – though I can't help feeling that they've already said all they have to say – but it can only be a fringe activity. If a band becomes successful, it's already seeking a larger audience than the folk world can provide, it's already using the language of rock (unless it's a rare bird indeed) and that language is an *extremely* restricted one in musical terms. Once you push experimentation a certain distance, there's little difference between musical styles – rock, jazz and 'classical' experiments all sound depressingly alike. And so you merely lose identity. You can't go on without changing, it simply isn't possible. And therefore you run into an impasse: you can't go forward and you can't go back. In that situation you can only stagnate – as we've already seen quite a few times.

With the contemporary singer–songwriter, then?

The presence of the singer–songwriter has always been more a symptom of folk's eclecticism – both in traditional and present-day terms – than a central part. There are good reasons for his being there, but it's not and never has been the basic driving force. In any case, there are simply far too few *good* songwriters to carry the weight of the burden.

So it's down to folksong per se?

Basically, it always has been. There are close parallels with jazz, you know. Both started out as minority cults, both have spread. Jazz started out a good time before the Folk Revival got going – over fifty years earlier – and twenty-five years or so into *its* history it was still hitting a lot of heavy weather. But it's settled now – a lot more settled than the Revival. It's accepted by a far larger part of the world's population, too. If you agree that the BBC largely reflects public taste, then it's significant that they put out a lot more jazz than they do folk – simply because there's a greater demand for it.

But that doesn't alter the fact that they're allied sub-cultures, both deriving from various traditional musics. They both play, in the main, to small to medium audiences; they both have problems in communication to the world at large; they both have knowledgeable and involved fans – they're definitely in-crowds, both of them.

It doesn't seem unlikely to me that in a few years' time folk will be in much the same position that jazz is in today: a generally accepted, specialist sector of musical entertainment, largely outside the in-fighting of the popular music world, and with its own serious intentions and achievements lying alongside the more light-hearted aspects. Some of Ellington's compositions, or some of those of Thelonius Monk or even Albert Ayler, are a long way in intention and fulfilment from 'Muskrat Ramble' or 'Petite Fleur' – though they all come from the same stable.

Similarly, folk should look to broadening its base – it's beginning to do it gradually now, as it finds its feet (for twenty-five years is not a long time) – and going outside itself. Going for a larger audience is not *necessarily* the same as going for the biggest possible audience, and compromise doesn't *necessarily* rear its ugly head to anything like the same degree. As jazz has proved, it's possible to operate on various levels without either damaging the music or losing personal integrity. In any case, folk music has been around for a hell of a long time now, and *it* won't die whatever happens to the Revival. But I tell you one thing.

Yes?

The sooner we lose this word 'Revival' the better. It's long outlived its usefulness.

Index

Gaughan, Dick, 25, 63–4, 72, 100
Glasgow, Alex, 106
Giltrap, Gordon, 71
Goulder, Dave, 110, 113–14
Gow, Neil, 44
Graebe, Martin, 25, 121
Graham, Davey, 71, 97
Grainger, Percy, 13, 16, 19, 24, 26, 28
Grimsby Folk Club, 88
Gryphon, 96
Guillory, Isaac, 71
Gummere, F. B., 23
Guthrie, Woody, 54, 106, 120

Haley, Bill, 51
Handle, Johnny, 81
Hands, Owen, 59
Harding, Mike, 66
Hardman, Rosemary, 117
Hardy, Thomas, 36
Harris, Roy, 66
Hart, Bob, 37
Hart, Tim, 98
Hatch, Tony, 108
Haynes, Mary Ann, 37
Headington Morris, 46
Heaney, Joe, 40
Hedgehog Pie, 66, 68
Henderson, Hamish, 83
Hickland, Tom, 45
High Level Ranters, The, 68, 73, 81
Higgins, Lizzie, 27, 39
Hinchcliffe, Frank, 34, 37, 82
Horslips, 66, 99
Howes, Frank, 21–2
Hughes, Herbert, 13
Hugill, Stan, 36
Hutchings, Ashley, 98, 99–100

Industrial Revolution, 14, 20, 101
Ives, Burl, 54

James, John, 71
Jansch, Bert, 71, 99
John Babbacombe Lee, 118
Johnson, Bob, 98
Jones, Nic, 61, 63, 68, 71, 72, 124
Jordan, Fred, 24, 27, 33, 35–6, 80

JSD Band, The, 66, 99

Karpeles, Maud, 28, 78
Kelly, Stan, 59
Kemp, Rick, 98
Kennedy, Peter, 19, 26, 78–9
Kennedy Fraser, Margaret, 13, 78
Kent, Enoch, 59
Kerr, Sandra, 74
Kettlewell, David, 74
Kidson, Frank, 13
Kiessewetter, Knut, 69
Killen, Louis, 58, 61, 74
Kimber, William, 46, 47
King of Elfland's Daughter, The, 118
Kingston Trio, 55
Kipling, Rudyard, 119
Kirkpatrick, John, 73–4, 100
Kitchen, Mervyn, 37
Kitchener, Lord, 56
Knight, Peter, 72, 98
Knudsen, Thorkild, 83

Laine, Frankie, 51
Larner, Sam, 18, 30, 34
Laycock, Tim, 124
Leadbelly, 54
Leader Records, 26, 80, 82, 84
Lewis, Bob, 37
Lewis, Jerry Lee, 51
Liege and Lief, 97–8
Lightfoot, Gordon, 108
Limeliters, The, 55
Lindisfarne, 66
Lloyd, A. L., 20, 21, 56, 57, 106
Lomax, Alan, 56
Love, Death and the Lady, 96
Lyons, Barry, 99

McAndrew, Hector, 44, 47
MacBeath, Jimmy, 39, 83
MacColl, Ewan, 20, 21, 25, 27, 39–40, 55–7, 59, 61, 83, 87, 105–6, 121–3
McCulloch, Geordanna, 66
McDevitt, Chas, 53
MacDonald, Mrs Archie, 38
MacDonald, Murdina, 38